William Goode

Rome's tactics

A lesson for England from the past

William Goode

Rome's tactics
A lesson for England from the past

ISBN/EAN: 9783337104344

Printed in Europe, USA, Canada, Australia, Japan

Cover: Foto ©ninafisch / pixelio.de

More available books at **www.hansebooks.com**

ROME'S TACTICS;

OR,

A LESSON FOR ENGLAND FROM THE PAST:

SHOWING THAT

THE GREAT OBJECT OF POPERY SINCE THE REFORMATION

HAS BEEN TO SUBVERT AND RUIN

PROTESTANT CHURCHES AND PROTESTANT STATES,

BY

Dissensions and Troubles caused by Disguised Popish Agents:

WITH A BRIEF NOTICE OF

𝕽ome's 𝔄llies in the 𝕮hurch of 𝕰ngland.

BY THE
VERY REV. WILLIAM GOODE, D.D., F.S.A.,

LATE DEAN OF RIPON.

WITH A PREFACE BY THE
VERY REV. HUGH McNEILE, D.D.,

DEAN OF RIPON.

LONDON:
THE CHRISTIAN BOOK SOCIETY,
22, KING WILLIAM STREET, STRAND, W.C.

1868.

PREFACE.

By the Council of the Christian Book Society, I am requested to write a few lines, introductory to a Cheap Edition of this admirable Tract. I rejoice in the opportunity thus afforded me to bear my humble and hearty testimony to the erudition, the accuracy, the Protestant zeal, the controversial acumen, and the Christian charity, of my highly valued and sincerely lamented predecessor, DEAN GOODE.

His was the watchful eye, and his the warning voice on the walls of our Zion, and it is well that by the circulation broadcast of the following pages, that voice should be heard reverberating throughout the land, at this crisis in our history.

Solomon said, " Surely in vain the net is spread in the sight of any bird." Dean Goode tore off Rome's mask, and exposed " ROME'S TACTICS." And to England he says, " Deliver thyself as a roe from the hand of the hunter, and as a bird from the snare of the fowler."

English Protestants are unsuspecting and uncombined because they are free. Their responsibility is personal, and the cultivation of *personal* responsibility is inseparable from a corresponding cultivation of independence of thought and feeling. This is one inevitable result of the free and dutiful exercise of private judgment; and as every one, individually, must give account of himself at the judgment-seat of Christ, it is right and proper that every one, individually, should think for himself now. As there will be no vicarious religion then, (except in Christ Himself,) so there ought to be none now. No mortal can answer for another then, therefore none should dare to do so now. This constitutes the excellence of our condition, as self-examining Christians; but this very excellence constitutes a main part of our exposure to the machinations of such a conspiracy as Romanism. Its object is supremacy over the souls and bodies of men. Its means are unscrupulous. Its organisation is complete. Where force can be used with safety and effect, it may—where fraud with better hope of success, it may—where a combination of both, it may. The canon law lays bishops, and through them, their priests, under an obligation to endeavour by all means, to obtain ASCENDANCY. For this purpose, having brought their "*subjects*" into a state of convenient vassalage, they employ them in divers disingenuous missions among Protestants—to foment disunion, to suggest doubt, to discourage reliance on the Bible, by insinuating uncertainty as to its canon, and obscurity as to its contents.

In a country like this, containing a teeming population, to thousands of whom we have no adequate means of extending the blessings of true Christian teaching, there must always be a large number of persons open to the machinations of such a body as the drilled agents of a Romish hierarchy.

Those agents are employed skilfully, according to their several qualifications for fraud or force, for perfidy or audacity, to unsettle the foundations of heretic society. Noisy bullies are employed to interrupt Protestant meetings, and prevent freedom of speech; swearing before magistrates that a breach of the peace is to be apprehended, a breach which they themselves have prepared and are ready to perpetrate. Sisters of charity are employed to commend themselves to the good graces of unwary and indigent Protestants, by visits of sympathy and invitations to cheap or even gratuitous education for their children. Writers of tales and catechisms are employed to captivate and indoctrinate the youthful mind. Poets and musicians are employed to gratify the taste, and entrance the senses.

Nor does the plan of the campaign end here. Witnesses are suborned and party confederacy prevails, to defeat the course of justice. And simultaneous combinations, with intent to intimidate, act in divers localities, with all the precision and punctuality of a disciplined army, while no man sees the officers in command.

Romanism has seldom of late years been regarded steadily under its genuine aspect of an unappeasable foe to civil liberty. In many senses a cheat, it is in every sense a tyrant. In vague and abstract terms, Rome professes to confine her jurisdiction to things spiritual: but in practice, by vigilant and subtle induction, by claims of relationship between things spiritual and things temporal, she brings all the affairs of this world within her constructive empire. In the council-room, in the confessional, in the closet, in the chamber, in the streets—ever watchful, ever menacing, ever exacting, ever calculating; where Popery through her ministers finds admission, there is no security, no confidence, no free agency, no free speech, no bold nor independent thought—all is unconscious, unvarying, irretrievable bondage.

What Mr. Wise, in his "History of the (Roman) Catholic Association" says of that most cunningly devised confederacy, may with truth be said of the entire machinery by which a Popish hierarchy assails a Protestant community:—" It was designed to tell ministers, in a language which could no longer be misunderstood, that, whenever the Association chose to call, there were the people ready to follow; that obedience to the Association was the paramount principle in the heart of every peasant in the country; that the power of the Association was therefore absolute and universal; that it could not be got rid of by the law, because it never infringed the law; that it could not be got rid of by brute force, because it never rendered brute force necessary; that it was therefore unattackable and enduring—that unattackable itself, it could attack others ; that, without injuring existing institutions, it might make use of those very institutions for every purpose of injury; that it could wield the constitution against the constitution; introduce a sullen, perpetual war into the bosom of peace ; disturb every relation of society, without violating a single enactment on which such relations repose ; and finally, produce such an order of things as to compel the minister to choose between coercion and conciliation."

This is frank, except the last word. Mr. Wise knew perfectly well that conciliation was out of the question. The choice left to the British Government was, and is, coercion or *submission*. It is on this issue that our senators should learn wisdom. Self-defence by law against such a system, is not intolerance. To treat such a system as if it were merely a religious difference, and not also a political conspiracy, is infatuation. To exclude from offices of *power* and *trust* in the state all who refuse to abjure such a conspiracy, is nothing more than common prudence. England may rest assured that her choice is narrowed to the painful, but inevitable alternative of exclusion or submission. Fair participation is utterly impracticable. Equality, the *beau ideal* of Liberalism, is spurned with supreme contempt by Rome. What! equality between the laws of the Vicar of Christ and the laws of a mere layman, especially an excommunicated heretic! The very thought is profane. No! *supremacy there must be, and England must either keep it for her own Sovereign, or yield it to a foreigner.* The foe are at the door ; and their archiepiscopal leader has told us with a loud voice that the Royal supremacy is no more, and has thereupon summoned us to surrender. How long will England patiently endure such insults, and continue to lick the hand that smites her?

But justice is the cry, justice between man and man ; and we are threatened with what continental nations say of our injustice. In answer to what has been said, and ably said, on that subject, by some of our (school) master spirits, I venture to think that justice between man and man in peace, is not justice between Rome and England. Justice implies fair play with reference to a common standard of right. Between Rome and England there is no common standard. England's aim is equal liberty to all. Rome's aim is absolute dominion over all. There can be no peace between them, except on one condition, and that to the utter exclusion of justice. Rome's unalterable condition is unconditional submission. Lord Arundel said truly in the House of Commons, (if not in these words, yet certainly to this effect,) "The antagonism is interminable, till one or other is subdued." What then is justice between army and army in the field? There must be victory before there can be peace. And after victory, if peace is to be permanent, precautions must be taken against mutiny and rebellion. England gained a victory, and took precautions. The land had rest two hundred years. England relaxed her precautions; and although the mutiny has begun, she refuses to defend herself, on the plea that it would be inconsistent in her to resume her former attitude. For the honour of consistency she is relaxing her precautions more and more, and dreaming of conciliation and harmony, while the mutiny, aided and abetted by traitors in the camp, is gathering strength for a rebellion. At the last, in spite of all her love of peace and offers of peace, and all her eloquent and learned eulogiums on justice and equality, she will be compelled either to fight or yield; either to be grossly inconsistent, or abjectly servile.

The issue, as Dean Goode has well said, " seriously affects the interests of others besides members of the Church of England." Rome, in the complicated struggle for ascendancy, plausibly joins in the cry for justice and equality; and gladly avails herself of auxiliaries in the non-conforming communions of our country. These, let it be frankly admitted, have too much cause for irritation and complaint. The tone concerning them, of some of our high Churchmen, is as unchristian as that of Rome herself: and it is not unreasonable that they should loathe and resent, as proof of connivance in high places, the growth, the unchecked growth, in our National Church, of superstitious novelties— not primitive practices, long neglected and now revived; but mediæval corruptions and puerilities which should never have been adopted.

In the face of all this, and deploring and condemning it as sincerely and as loudly as they do; we yet venture respectfully to remonstrate with any among them who feel tempted to desert us in the contest. Look at the alternative. If there be whips in the Church of England, there are scorpions in the Church of Rome. The whips are removable. The Protestant people of England can do it. The millions still sound in the National Church, and the millions still orthodox in the dissenting communions, have but to restrain their superficial jealousies which reach nothing vital, and speak out with one voice, and the National Church can be cleansed. But the scorpions are irremoveable. Rome in her infallibility is unchangeable, and in her supremacy, if attained, would not endure any dissent. In the plenitude of her power, her simple and only formula for all Nonconformists is " *ex nolente, fiat volens.*"

Even as a choice of evils then, to which we are often reduced in this world, you should all be with us. But this appeal is made much stronger, and much more prevailing with the best and noblest among you, when we remind you, that notwithstanding all our practical defections, we still hold, and hold fast, that precious deposit of Scriptural truth, and the sufficiency of the Scripture which teaches it, in defence of which our common forefathers bled and burned, rather than adopt the traditions, or even connive at the idolatries of the Church of Rome.

For the Christian Church, in the highest and best sense of the term, we entertain no apprehensions. We know in whom we have believed. We know Him who said, " Fear not, little flock, it is your Father's good pleasure to give you the kingdom." And again, "All that the Father giveth to me shall come to me, and him that cometh to me I will in no wise cast out." "I give unto them eternal life, and they shall never perish, neither shall any man pluck them out of my hand. My Father which gave them me is greater than all, and no man shall be able to pluck them out of my Father's hand. I and my Father are one."

Yes, for the members of Christ's mystical body, the bride, the Lamb's wife, the blessed company of all faithful people, we fear nothing, and have nothing to fear. The promises of God to them are all yea and all amen in Christ Jesus. Neither the gates of hell nor the machinations of antichrist can prevail against any one of them. Their hallelujahs shall ascend before the Throne when the smoke of the torments of the beast and the false prophet shall also ascend. "Babylon the great is fallen, is fallen! And her smoke rose up for ever and ever." "And much people in heaven sang Hallelujah, salvation and glory and honour and power unto the Lord our God!"

But we have no such promise for our beloved country. The golden candlestick of pure and Scriptural Christianity may be removed from England, as it has been from other lands—and we confess we have not become so transcendental nor so cosmopolitan as to have abjured all Christian Patriotism. If this be a weakness in the eyes of abstract philosophy, we must plead guilty to it. Patriotism is permitted—nay, it is to be cultivated—in the followers of Him who wept over corrupt and doomed Jerusalem; and England is called, and loudly called, to the decision and energy essential to the present crisis, in the name, the sacred, the animating name of Christian Patriotism. Christian Patriotism! the most touching and, next to the love of God in Christ, the noblest passion of the human heart—the love, the undying love of that country which protected the cradles of our infancy, and encloses the ashes of our fathers; the happy scene of childhood, when all was hope and joy; when innocence was in every heart, and pleasure in every eye; when every smile was bliss, and every thought was buoyant

A

rapture; when a father's benignant encouragement, a mother's affectionate embrace, a sister's softening and humanising companionship, conveyed to the ripening character indelible impressions of philanthrophy—impressions associated for ever with the walks, the trees, the rivers, the mountains, amongst which the gentle influences twined themselves round the yet plastic soul. Christian Patriotism! " the holy romance of sensibility and virtue." Free-born Englishmen, be wise, be firm. Ye thousands who are now for the first time to be invested with a share in political responsibility, be wise, be firm. Deliver your country, your beloved country, unequalled on the globe—oh, deliver her, and keep her delivered, decidedly, and no mistake, from the despotic grasp of antichrist, from the snares and ambuscades of Rome's Tactics, from the iron chain of Rome's Canon Law.

The Deanery, Ripon,
September, 1868.

ROME'S TACTICS.

&c. &c.

The subversion of Protestantism has been the great object to which the efforts of the Church of Rome have been directed, from the Reformation in the sixteenth century to the present day. And the mode in which it has been sought to accomplish this object, has been suitable to the character of that corrupt system for whose defence it was required. As soon as a purer form of faith and worship had taken such firm root in Europe that no hope remained of extirpating it by direct persecution, the resolution was immediately taken at Rome to attempt its destruction, in the countries where it prevailed, by sowing the seeds of dissension among its adherents, chiefly by sending among them teachers of *all kinds of false and antagonistic views and doctrines*, both civil and ecclesiastical, and thus producing a state of moral confusion in the country, and preventing any harmonious action in Church or State. Rome clearly saw that there was no surer way of preventing the growth and influence of that teaching that threatened her very life. So far as she could secure mutual hostility among the various Protestant Communions, and especially *internal discord*, so far would their power to propagate those all-important doctrines of the Christian faith, the light of which God had through their means restored to the world, revealing the true character of the religion of the Church of Rome, be paralysed. And the hope was cherished, that when a state of disquiet and dissension had been produced, the voice of the Church of Rome would be recognized as alone able to restore peace, and by its authority terminate the strife.

For the accomplishment of this purpose no mode of action has been more in favour with that corrupt politico-ecclesiastical body than the employment of *disguised agents* playing a double part and carrying on secret operations for the purpose of producing confusion and discord, and consequent ruin, in Protestant Churches and States. Dispensations have always been freely to be had at Rome for the assumption of any character, and the prosecution of any scheme of hypocrisy, fraud, or even violence, by which Protestantism was likely to suffer, and the interests of the Church of Rome might be promoted.

So little, however, is generally known of the artifices of Rome in this respect—*artifices to which, it must be recollected, we are quite as much exposed at the present day as at any former period*—that I think it may be useful to bring before the public a few evidences of the nature of her practices in this respect, drawn from the experience of former times. We are indebted, of course, for all the knowledge we have on the subject, to the *occasional* and *fortuitous* discovery of particular cases, which, notwithstanding the studious efforts at concealment, have through some peculiar contingency come to light; from which, however, our conclusions as to the *course* deliberately and systematically pursued by Rome are inevitable.

I shall confine myself, in the following pages, to what has taken place in this country; and limit the evidence adduced, so as to bring it within the compass of those who are too much engaged to read larger works.

And I believe it to be of vital importance to the best interests of Great Britain, both in Church and State, at the present time, that the dangers to which a Protestant country is exposed from this cause should be known.

That the present state of things among us is greatly due to the presence of innumerable Romish emissaries, many of them working under various disguises, and using half-hearted and ill-informed and weak Protestants as their tools, can hardly be denied by any one well-informed on such subjects. One testimony may suffice for proof. Some years since, an eminent foreign statesman stated to one from whom I had the information,—*We have got rid of the Jesuits as far as human power will enable any Government to get rid of such a body of men, but England is swarming with them, and before long you will feel the effects of their presence.*

The following pages will show what those effects are. And if the circumstances of the times may give a less *sanguinary* character to some of those effects, than they have had at some former periods, it must be remembered that their object is the same; the re-establishment of a system of anti-Christian superstition, in which the religion of Christ is turned into blind submission to a human priesthood, the spiritual worship of the Gospel Dispensation exchanged for a sensuous ceremonialism, and the consciences of men are enslaved to the dictates of one whose claim to infallibility is justly punished by his being permitted to lapse into errors and follies which the common sense of mankind repudiates. I shall give the evidence in chronological order.

In 1549 the following letter was sent to the Bishops of Winchester and Rochester. It was found by Sir Henry Sidney among Queen Mary's papers.

"Edward, son of Henry, the heretic King of England, by his crafty and politic Council hath absolutely brought in heresy, which if not by *art* or other endeavours speedily overthrown and made infamous, all other foreign heretics will unite with your new heresies now amongst yourselves lately planted, and so have bishops as you have; and it is the opinion of our learned men now at Trent that the schisms in England by Edward's Council established will reclaim all the foreign sects unto their discipline, and thereby be *one body united*. For Calvin, Bullinger, and others have wrote unto Edward to offer their service to assist and unite, also to make Edward and his heirs their chief defender, and so have bishops as well as England; which if it come to pass, that heretic bishops be so near and spread abroad, *Rome and the Clergy utterly falls. You must therefore make these offertures of theirs odious to Edward and his Council.* Receive N. S. and E. L. from Rotterdam; *their lessons are taught them; take you their parts, if checked by the other heretics;* for these be for rebaptising, and not for infant baptism. Their doctrine is for a future monarchy upon earth after death, *which will please the ordinary kind well, and dash the other that rageth now amongst you.* Reverend fathers, it is left to you to assist, and to those you know are sure to the Mother-Church. From Delph the 4th Ide of May, anno Christi, 1549. D. G."*

Sir H. Sidney says, that he showed this letter to Queen Elizabeth, "at the sight whereof she was startled, the letter being amongst her sister's papers, which caused her to express these very words: 'I had rather than a year's revenue, that my brother Edward and his Council had seen this letter; nay rather than twice my revenue *I had seen it sooner.*' "†

And in connection with this remark of Queen Elizabeth, which clearly showed how she believed herself to have been misled by similar practices, we may observe the remarkable testimony of Bishop Burnet, in a sermon which he preached in 1688 before the House of Commons.

" Here suffer me to tell you," he says, " that in the beginning of Queen Elizabeth's reign our adversaries saw no hopes of retrieving their affairs, which had been spoiled by Queen Mary's persecution, but by setting on foot *divisions among Protestants* upon very inconsiderable matters. I myself have seen the letters of the chief bishops of that time, from which it appears that the Queen's stiffness in maintaining some ceremonies flowed not from their Councils, but from the practices of some *disguised Papists.*"‡

In a Bull of Pope Paul the Third is granted the following indulgence:—

---

* Foxes and Firebrands, pt. 2, 1682. 8vo. pp. 11—13. This book was published by Robert Ware, son of Sir James Ware, to whom some of Cecil's papers came through the medium of Archbishop Usher, which supplied some of the most valuable documents he has here published.

† Ibid. p. 13.

‡ Bishop Burnet's Sermon before the House of Commons, January 31, 1688. London: 1689. 4to, pp. 14, 15.

"Whereas we find the heretics now concord in the administration of the sacrament of the body of Jesus, we grant full remission of sins to those our sons of our Mother-Church that shall stop or hinder *their union* amongst heretics."*

The following instructions were sent, in 1551, from the Council of Trent to the Jesuits of Paris, through Casa, Archbishop of Benevento. The report of these instructions rests upon the testimony of a convert from Romanism in 1566, of the name of Samuel Mason, who had been bred up with the Jesuits at Paris, and who, coming over to this country, was after his recantation appointed by Archbishop Adam Loftus to the cure of a parish near Dublin, where he died; Dr. Garvey, Dean of Christ Church, Dublin, and afterwards Archbishop of Armagh, preaching his funeral sermon. He says,—

"The messenger between the Council of Trent and the Jesuits of Paris, was Ludovick de Freake, formerly a priest in England, who brought with him up to Paris, from the Council, several kind of Indulgences and Instructions for the Society to undertake and grant and teach. Part of the Instructions were thus, To take notice of the confessions of the people of France, especially of the nobles and gentry; and in case they suspect anything detrimental to the Holy See of Rome, then to confer with three or more Confessors of the suspicion, and so to take memorandums of certain questions to be asked of the party so suspected the next time. Also to converse with the noblest, and to discourse variously until they find which way he is inclinable most, and to please them accordingly in their discourse; and in case any of you be, or chance to be, any of their Confessors, ye are to take memorandums of things doubtful and suspicious, and at the next Confession to urge them to those parties then confessing, by which any three or more are to consult, and give the See of Rome and her Councils intelligence more or less, that the Mother-Church might be informed, and all evil prevented that is or shall be pretended against her.

"You are to associate with all strangers, heretical, as well

* Foxes, &c., p. 24.

as Christian Catholic; if heretical, to be civil, *and not to discover your profession;* and for the better procurement of these designs, designed or to be accomplished, *ye may with leave of any three of the Society be permitted to wear what dress or habit you think convenient,* provided the Society hear from the party so dispensed. *Any of you thus dispensed with may go with the heretic to any of their heretical meetings* permitted by Acts or Contracts of peace between princes. By *this contrivance* ye may both inform the Mother-Church, and in case any of you be employed to assist her to go into any of the heretical villages or territories, you will be the more able to serve the Holy See of St. Peter, and *keep yourselves from suspicion.*

" In case any of you be thus employed, ye are dispensed with either to go with heretics to their churches, or as you see convenient. If you own yourselves clergymen, then to preach, but with caution, till ye be well acquainted with those heretics you converse with, and THEN BY DEGREES ADD TO YOUR DOCTRINE BY CEREMONIES, *or otherwise, as you find them inclinable.* If ye be known by any of the lay Catholics, you are to pacify them by saying secret Mass unto them, or by acquainting other priests (who are not able to undertake this work) with your intentions who doth [do] generally say Mass unto them. If the Laymen be of any parts, or of wit, you may dispense with them also, reserving the same provisoes, and thereby he may acquire an estate, and be the more able to serve the Mother-Church.

" In case they scruple in taking of oaths, you are to dispense with them, assuring them that they are to be *kept no longer than the Mother-Church sees it convenient;* or if they scruple to swear on the Evangelists, you are to say unto them, that the translation on which they swear his Holiness the Pope hath annulled, and *thereby it is become heretical, and all as one as upon an ordinary story-book.*

" In case in strange countries ye be known by merchants or others trading or travelling thither, for to strengthen your designs the more for your intention, you are dispensed with to marry after their manner, and then ye safely may make answer, that heretical marriage is no marriage ; for your Dispensation mollifies it so, that at the worst it is but a venial sin, and may be forgiven.

"Ye are not to preach all after one method, but to observe the place wherein you come. If Lutheranism be prevalent, then preach Calvinism; if Calvinism, then Lutheranism; if in England, then either of them, or John Huss's opinions, Anabaptism, or any that are contrary to the Holy See or [of] St. Peter, by which your function will not be suspected, and yet you may still act on the interest of the Mother-Church; THERE BEING, AS THE COUNCIL ARE AGREED ON, NO BETTER WAY TO DEMOLISH THAT CHURCH OF HERESY, BUT BY MIXTURES OF DOCTRINES, AND BY ADDING OF CEREMONIES MORE THAN BE AT PRESENT PERMITTED.

"SOME OF YOU WHO UNDERTOOK TO BE OF THIS SORT OF HERETICAL EPISCOPAL SOCIETY, BRING IT AS NEAR TO THE MOTHER-CHURCH AS YOU CAN; for then the Lutheran party, the Calvinists, the Anabaptists, and other heretics will be averse thereunto, and thereby make that Episcopal heresy odious to all these, and be a means to reduce all in time to the Mother Church.

"You are further (during the time you take these shapes upon you) to observe thus much of the rules of the Mother-Church. The Mother-Church disowneth the Regal Power to be her superior, especially the Heretical Powers Regal or otherwise. Upon this ye are to take these measures: you must bemoan your followers and auditors, saying, 'Are not we persecuted for righteousness' sake? What flesh and blood can endure this? We be more zealous against the Pope than they, and yet we be persecuted.' By these means your contrivances will light on those ye lead along and not on yourselves. This will advantage you much; hang you or burn you they dare not; but their perpetual acts against the party that follow you will take off the late severities they lay on us in saying, we burnt the heretics their ancestors; and so at last bring that odium upon that heretical Church in England, which they have thrown on us. And as you will be more admired by the people, so the heretics will asperse that heretical king and his church, as little differing from us.

"These Instructions I am commanded to recommend unto you, as being approved by his Holiness Julius the Third, your Supreme Father, and his wholesome Council, to be handled and performed to the utmost of your powers, wealth, parts, learning, and capacities, for the good of the Mother-Church. Dated the fourth Ide of November, 1551."*

During the reign of Mary there was of course no necessity for Romish agents acting under any disguise in this country. But almost immediately after the accession of Elizabeth we find them again at work.

Among Cecil's (Lord Burghley's) papers that came into the hands of Sir James Ware was a letter from a confidential agent of Queen Elizabeth, dated "Venice, April 13, 1564," enclosing an account of "several consultations amongst the Cardinals, Bishops, and others of the several Orders of Rome, now contriving and conspiring against her gracious Majesty and the Established Church of England," from which I give the following extracts:—

"Pius having consulted with the clergy of Italy and assembling them together, it was by general consent voted, that the immunity of the Romish Church and her jurisdiction is required to be defended by all her princes, as the principal Church of God. And to encourage the same, the Council hath voted that Pius should bestow Her Grace's realm on that Prince who shall attempt to conquer it. There was a Council ordered by way of a Committee, who contain three of the Cardinals, two of the Archbishops, six of the Bishops, and as many of the late Order of the Jesuits, who daily increase, and come into great favour with the Pope of late. These do present, weekly, methods, ways and contrivances, for the Church of Rome, which hold the great Council for the week following in employment how to order all things for the advancement of the Romish faith. Some of these contrivances coming to my hands by the help of the silver key, be as follow:—

"1. The people of England being much averted from

* Foxes, &c., pp. 27—33.

their Mother-Church of Rome, they have thought fit, sounding out their inclinations how the common sort are taken with the Liturgy in English, for to offer Her Grace to confirm it, with some things altered therein, provided that Her Grace and the Council do acknowledge the same from Rome and her Council; which if it be denied, as we suppose it will, then these are to asperse the Liturgy of England by all ways and conspiracies imaginable.

"2. A Licence or Dispensation to be granted to any of the Romish Orders to preach, speak, or write against the new Established Church of England, *amongst other protesters against Rome,* purposely to make England odious to them [*i.e.*, to the other protesters against Rome], and that they may retain their assistances promised them, in case of any Prince's invasion, and the parties so licenced and indulged (dispensed with) to be *seemingly as one of them,* and not to be either taxed checkt or excommunicated for so doing; and further, for the better assurance of the party so licenced and indulged, the party *to change his name lest he be discovered,* and to keep a quarternal correspondence with any of the Cardinals, Archbishops, Bishops, Abbots, Priors, or others of the chief Monasteries, Abbies, &c. At [? All] which quarternal correspondence shall not only give the Pope intelligence of heretical conspiracy, but be a full assurance of their fidelity to Rome. This proposal was much debated in the Council, which caused some of the Council to say, how shall we prevent it, in case any of the parties so licenced flinch from us, and receive a good reward, and fall off from our correspondency.

"3. It was then ordered that there should be several appointed for to watch the parties so licenced and indulged, and to give intelligence to Rome of their behaviour, which parties are sworn not to divulge to any of those so licenced or indulged what they be, or from whence they came, but *to be strange and to come in as one of their converts,* so that the party shall be cautious how and which way he bendeth.

"It was afterwards debated how it should be ordered in case any of the heretical ministry of England should become as they who had these Licences, and what should be done in that case.

4. "It was then answered by the Bishop of *Mens*, that *that was the thing they aimed at*, and that they desired no more than *separation amongst the heretics of England*, and by so doing, in case any animosity be amongst them, the Church established by the heretic Queen, (as they so termed Her Grace,) there would be *the less to oppose the Mother-Church of Rome*, whenever opportunity served. This reason of the Bishop pacified the whole Council.

"5. It was granted not only Indulgence and Pardon to the party that should assault Her Grace, either private or in public; or to any cook, brewer, baker, physician, vintner, grocer, chirurgion, or any other calling whatsoever, that should or did make her away out of this world, a pardon, but an absolute remission of sins to the heirs of that party's family sprung from him, and a perpetual annuity to them for ever, and the said heir to be never beholding to any of the Fathers for pardon, be they of what Order soever, unless it pleased himself, and to be one of those Privy-Council, whosoever reigned, successively.

"6. It was ordered for the better assurance of further intelligence to the See of Rome, to give Licences to any that shall swear to that Supremacy due obedience and allegiance to *her powers to dispense with sacraments, baptisms, marriages, and other ceremonies of our now Established Church in England, that the parties so obliged may possess and enjoy any office or employment, either ecclesiastical, military, or civil*, AND TO TAKE SUCH OATHS *as shall be imposed upon them, provided that the said oaths be taken with a reserve for to serve the Mother-Church of Rome whenever opportunity serveth, and thereby, in so doing, the Act of Council was passed,* IT WAS NO SIN, BUT MERITORIOUS, *until occasion served to the contrary; and that when it was so served for Rome's advantage, the party was absolved from his oath.*"

[Here follow other directions to the Romish party in England to do " what in them lieth for the promotion of the

Romish cause," to "propose a match for the Queen of the Catholic Princes," and pronouncing "a perpetual curse" on all those who "will not promote" "Mary Queen of Scotland's pretence to the Crown of England," &c.]

"11. It is ordered that the See of Rome do *dispense with all parties of the Roman faith to swear against all heretics of England as elsewhere, and that not to be a crime or an offence against the soul of the party, the accuser taking the oath with an intention to promote or advance the Roman Catholic faith.*"*

In 1566, a Bull of Anathema against the Protestants was issued by Pope Pius the Fifth, in the first year of his pontificate, in which he exhorts the wise and learned of his ecclesiastics to "endeavour and devise all manner of devices to be devised to abate, assuage, and confound those heresies repugnant to our sacred laws, that thereby these heretics might be either recalled to confess their errors, and acknowledge our jurisdiction of the See of Rome, or that a *total infamy may be brought upon them and their posterities by a perpetual* DISCORD AND CONTENTION *amongst themselves*, by which means they may either speedily perish by God's wrath, or *continue in* ETERNAL DIFFERENCE, to the reproach [scandal] of Jew, Turk, heathen, &c."†

Accordingly we find well-authenticated instances of Romish emissaries coming to this country and acting upon these principles.

In 1567, a man who went by the name of Faithful Commin, afterwards found to be a Dominican friar, but professing to be a zealous Protestant, and who had endeavoured to promote religious dissensions in this country, was brought before the Queen's Council on suspicion of his being a concealed Romanist.

An account of his examination before the Council is given from Lord Burghley's papers in the work already quoted, and he pleaded that he had "spoken against Rome and her Pope as much as any of the clergy had since they had fallen from

---

* Foxes, &c., pp. 51—58.
† Ibid. p. 41. See also Strype's Annals, ch. 48, vol. i. pt. 2. p. 218. (Oxf. ed.)

her," and "wondered why he should be suspected." But having been let off on bail, he managed to escape, telling his deluded followers that "he was warned of God to go beyond the seas to instruct the Protestants there," getting thirty pounds from them for his support on his travels. And having made his way to Rome and informed the Pope what he had been doing, and that he had raised a spirit in some of the people against the Church of England that would be "*a stumbling-block to that Church while it is a Church*," was "commended" by "His Holiness" for his labours, and received from him "a reward of 2000 ducats for his good service."*

In the following year (1568) a similar case was discovered in the Diocese of Rochester; an account of which is given in the same work, as copied from "the Registry of the Episcopal See of Rochester in that Book which begins anno 2 & 3 Phil. & Mary, and continued to 15 Eliz."

From this account it appears, that Thomas Heth, a concealed Jesuit, brother of Nicholas Heth, who had been Bishop of Rochester and afterwards Archbishop of York, labouring to sow dissensions among the English Protestants, having been allowed to preach in Rochester Cathedral, was detected by a letter which he accidentally dropped in the pulpit addressed to him by a leading Jesuit at Madrid. In this letter, dated Madrid, Oct. 1568, after stating that "the Council" of the Fraternity had sent him some books for distribution, and adding, "these mixtures with your own will not only a little puzzle the understandings of the auditors, but make yourself famous," the writer says, "Hallingham Coleman and Benson have *set a faction among the German heretics*, so that several who have turned from us have now denied their baptism, which we hope will soon turn the scale and bring them back to their old principles. This we have certified to the Council and Cardinals, That there is no other way to prevent people from turning heretics

---

* Foxes and Firebrands, pt. 1. pp. 14—29. And Strype's Life of Parker, vol. i. pp. 485—488. Oxf. ed.

and for the recalling of others back again to the Mother-Church than by *the diversities of doctrines.*"*

And upon searching Heth's lodgings, there was found "a licence from the Fraternity of the Jesuits, and a Bull dated the first of Pius Quintus to preach what doctrine that Society pleased for *the dividing of Protestants*, particularly naming the English Protestants by the name of heretics."†

In 1580 came over to this country Parsons and Campian, of whom our historian Fuller says:—"These two effectually advanced the Roman cause, appearing in more several shapes than Proteus himself, in the disguised habits of soldiers, courtiers, ministers of the word, apparitors, as they were advised by their profit and safety; and as if his Holiness had infused an ubiquitariness into them, they acted in city, court and country."‡

Campian's mode of proceeding is best testified by a letter of his own to the General of the Jesuits, intercepted by Walsingham, which is printed by Fuller, in which, after giving an account how he deceived the parties who questioned him on his landing, he states how he secretly exercised his ministry and administered the sacraments, adding, —"In the administering of them we are assisted by the priests, whom we find everywhere;" and says, "*I am in a most antick habit, which I often change, as also my name.*" —"Eminent work we have effected; innumerable number of converts, high, low, of the middle rank, of all ages and sexes."—"By wariness and the prayers of good people, and (which is the main) by God's goodness, we have in safety gone over a great part of the Island."§

Our quaint but truthful historian Fuller, after giving a particular account of the cases of Parsons and Campian, adds generally, under the same year, 1580,—"Now began priests and Jesuits to flock faster into England than ever

---

* Foxes and Firebrands, pt. 1. 2nd ed., London, 1682, 8vo, pp. 37—39.
† Ibid. pp. 40, 41. The whole account is taken from the Episcopal Registry of Rochester.
‡ Fuller's Church History, Book ix. Sect. iii. § 41.
§ Ibid.

before; *having exchange of clothes and names and professions.* He who on Sunday was a priest or Jesuit, was on Monday a merchant, on Tuesday a soldier, on Wednesday a courtier, &c.; and, with *the shears of equivocation* (constantly carried about him), he could cut himself into any shape he pleased. But under all their new shapes they retained their old nature, being akin in their turbulent spirits to the wind pent in the subterranean concavities, which *will never be quiet until it hath vented itself with a* STATE-QUAKE *of those countries wherein they abide.* These distilled traitorous principles into all people wheresoever they came, and endeavoured to render them disaffected to Her Majesty, maintaining, that she neither had nor ought to have any dominion over her subjects, while she persisted in an heretical distance from the Church of Rome."*

A similar case, occurring in the Diocese of Norwich in 1584, is related in the Book of Memorials of matters of this kind kept by Cecil, Lord Burghley, that came into the hands of Sir James Ware, as above stated. It was discovered through a letter found in the possession of Francis Throgmorton, a Papist apprehended for treason in London in 1584. And among the papers found in Throgmorton's chamber "were Licenses and Pardons from the Jesuits' Convent at Seville: the undertakers were to be of what trade or calling soever they pleased, *to teach what doctrine, to be of what opinion or religion soever,* provided that they assembled quarterly together, and kept a monthly correspondence with that Convent." This Francis Throgmorton "before his execution confessed that there were in England above a dozen that he knew who were permitted to preach by the Jesuits' Licences, purposely to breed a faction in these dominions."†

I pass over, as of a somewhat different character, the various plots in which the Romanists were engaged during the whole of Queen Elizabeth's reign to take away her life; plots for which they had the direct and express sanction and encourage-

---

* Fuller's Church History, Book ix. Sect. iv. § 6.
† Foxes and Firebrands, pt. 2, pp. 58—61.

ment of the Court of Rome; and of which a full account is given by Foulis in his "History of Romish Treasons and Usurpations" (2nd edition, London, 1681, fol.) Book vii. pp. 311—360. And on the same ground I shall omit any account of the Gunpowder Plot at the commencement of the reign of James I., of which a description may be found in various works, and among others in that just quoted, Book x.

These plots afford an awful illustration of the real character and spirit of Popery. But I am now more particularly directing attention to that species of Papal agency which was carried on through disguised agents working deceitfully to effect their ends through the instrumentality of others, by misleading the minds of men, and producing a state of moral confusion in the country.

The efforts of Rome for the subversion of Protestantism were unceasingly carried on in the same way during the next century. Various cases of dispensed priests and Jesuits, both in England and Ireland, accidentally discovered under the disguise they had assumed, professing to be Protestants, but labouring to discredit and divide the Church of England, one as a shoemaker, another as a soldier, and others of a similar kind, are given in the work from which I have so largely quoted above.*

And it is clear, from the documents here adduced, that their efforts to produce ecclesiastical dissensions went hand in hand with similar efforts to cause discord and confusion in the State. "Heretical" Kings and Governments, as the supporters of "heretical" Churches, were equally the objects of Papal hatred with the ecclesiastical systems which they upheld. The agents of Rome, therefore, were as diligent in their endeavours to undermine the one as the other, and the great instrument they made use of for both was the excitement of a spirit of strife and discord. Regardless of the moral nature of the doctrines and principles they advocated, their

* Foxes and Firebrands, Pt. 2, pp. 98—101, 102—104, &c.

B

sole object was to break up both Church and State into a number of opposite parties, all contending with one another, and so producing a chaos of confusion, out of which they hoped to emerge triumphant. And they were carefully trained in their foreign seminaries to act under all sorts of disguises in the carrying out of this nefarious project; some acting their part more especially in strictly ecclesiastical matters, others in matters affecting the State, and others, the more talented among them, in both departments of labour.

An intercepted letter from a Jesuit in London to his correspondent at Brussels, from which the following are extracts, was sent, in 1627, to Lord Falkland, the Lord Deputy of Ireland, by four of the leading members of the Privy Council in London, to inform him of the secret doings of the Papists.

"Let not the damp of astonishment seize upon your ardent and zealous soul in apprehending the sudden and unexpected calling of a Parliament. We have not opposed but rather furthered it. So that we hope as much in this Parliament as ever we feared any in Queen Elizabeth's days. . . . . You shall see this Parliament will resemble the Pelican, which takes a pleasure to dig out with her beak her own bowels." The letter goes on to state how Count Gondomar deluded King James in order to further the projected Spanish match for Prince Charles, and tried to persuade him " that none but the *Puritan Faction*, which plotted nothing but anarchy and his confusion, were averse to this most happy union ;" proceeding thus,—" We steered on the same course . . . . and have prejudicated and anticipated the Great One, that *none but the King's enemies and his are chosen of this Parliament*. . . . . Now we have planted that sovereign drug Arminianism, which we hope will purge the Protestants from their heresy ; and it flourisheth and bears fruit in due season. *The materials which build up our bulwark are the projectors and beggars of all ranks and qualities.* Howsoever, both these Factions co-operate to destroy the Parliament, and to introduce a **new species and form of government, which is oligarchy**. Those serve as direct mediums and instruments to our end, which is THE UNIVERSAL CATHOLIC MONARCHY. *Our foundation must be mutation, and mutation will cause a relaxation, which will serve as so many violent diseases, &c.* .... There is another matter of consequence, which we take much into our consideration and tender care, which is *to stave off Puritans*, that they hang not in the Duke's ears; they are impudent subtle people. And it is to be feared lest they should negotiate a reconciliation between the Duke and the Parliament at Oxford and Westminster; but now we assure ourselves, *we have so handled the matter, that both Duke and Parliament are irreconcileable.* For the better prevention of the Puritans, the Arminians have already locked up the Duke's ears, and we have those of our own religion, which stand continually at the Duke's chamber to see who goes in and out. We cannot be too circumspect and careful in this regard. *I cannot choose but laugh to see how some of our own coat have accoutered themselves, you would scarce know them if you saw them.* And it is admirable how in speech and gesture they *act the Puritans*. The Cambridge scholars, to their woeful experience, shall see we can act the Puritans a little better than they have done the Jesuits. They have abused our sacred patron St. Ignatius in jest; but we will make them smart for it in earnest."*

Among the papers of Archbishop Usher it appears from this work† that there were several documents showing the various methods "contrived by the clergy and others of the Romish Church to nullify the Reformation of the Church of England," some of which are there given under the title of —"The Oath of Secrecy devised by the Roman Clergy, as it remaineth on record at Paris, amongst the Society of Jesus; together with several Dispensations and Indulgences granted to all pensioners of the Church of Rome, who disguisedly undertake to propagate the faith of the Church of Rome, and her advancement. Faithfully translated out of French."

* Ibid. Pt. 2, pp. 118—128. Rushworth's Historical Collections, vol. i. pp. 474—476.   † Pt. 3, p. 171.

The "Oath of Secrecy" "framed in the Papacy of Urban VIII." about the year 1636, was as follows:—

"I, A. B., now in the presence of Almighty God, the Blessed Virgin Mary, the Blessed Michael the Archangel, the Blessed St. John Baptist, the holy Apostles St. Peter and St. Paul, and the Saints and Sacred Host of Heaven, and to you my ghostly Father, do declare from my heart, without mental reservation, That His Holiness Pope Urban is Christ's Vicar-General, and is the true and only Head of the Catholic or Universal Church throughout the earth; and that by the virtue of the keys of binding and loosing given to His Holiness by my Saviour Jesus Christ, he hath power to depose heretical kings, princes, states, commonwealths, and governments, all being illegal without his sacred confirmation, and that they may safely be destroyed. Therefore to the utmost of my power I shall and will defend this doctrine and His Holiness's rights and customs against all usurpers of the heretical (or Protestant) authority whatsoever; especially against the now pretended authority and Church of England, and all adherents, in regard that they and she be usurpal and heretical, opposing the sacred Mother-Church of Rome. I do renounce and disown any allegiance as due to any heretical king prince or state, named Protestants, or obedience to any of their inferior magistrates or officers. I do further declare, That the doctrine of the Church of England, of the Calvinists, Hugonots, and of other of the name Protestants, to be [is] damnable, and they themselves are damned, and to be damned, that will not forsake the same. I do further declare, That I will help, assist, and advise all or any of His Holiness's agents in any place, wherever I shall be, in England Scotland and Ireland, or in any other territory or kingdom I shall come to; and do my utmost to extirpate the heretical Protestants' doctrine, and to destroy all their pretended power *regal or otherwise.* I do further promise and declare, That notwithstanding *I am dispensed with to assume any religion heretical for the propagating of the Mother-Church's interest,* to keep secret and private all her agents' counsels from time to time, as they intrust me, and not to divulge directly or indirectly, by word, writing, or circumstance, whatsoever, but to *execute all what shall be proposed, given in charge or discovered unto me*, by you my ghostly Father, or by any of this Sacred Convent [*i.e.* Assembly]. All which I, A. B., do swear by the blessed Trinity and blessed Sacrament, which I now am to receive, to perform, and on my part to keep inviolably: and do call all the heavenly and glorious host of heaven to witness these my real intentions to keep this my oath. In testimony hereof I take this most holy and blessed sacrament of the Eucharist; and witness the same further with my hand and seal in the face of this holy Convent this . . . day of . . . . an. Dom. &c."*

Among the same papers were various regulations and orders proposed by the Jesuits and Sorbonists at Paris, and agreed to by the Pope and Cardinals at Rome, after the marriage of King Charles I. with the daughter of the King of France, for the promotion of the cause of the Church of Rome in England. Among these regulations were the following :—

"Seeing that laws are made in England that none of the Mother-Church members must be capable of great or small employments, or places of any trust; it is requisite to *grant dispensations to divers parties* to go to church, yet to take the oath as aforesaid, be he pensioner, be he officer, thus dispensed with; the party confessing quarterly or monthly as the confessor shall urge the party, and to receive the eucharist at the confession during this dispensation; and *secretly inform the Mother-Church's agents of causes, matters and affairs accordingly.*"

"That the parties employed *to multiply the divisions amongst heretics*, there being no other way to confound their heresies, seeing grace nor reason will not avert them from the same, *must be dispensed with to rail outwardly against us, yet against the heresies of the Church of England, comparing them to us, and so rail against our Church, thereby only to in-*

* Pt. 3, pp. 172—175.

crease the division amongst heretics. This alteration [or, mutability] of heresy will convert many to the Mother-Church, beholding their inconstancy, and also hinder weak Romanists from changing their faith to heresy, *we underhand preaching it as a judgment of God, fallen upon heretics, called Protestants, to fall from the Mother-Church.*"

"That the money raised for pensioners to keep of [off] acts, wars, *to discover all counsels of heretic princes and states, to infuse matters into their brains,* and to carry on the Roman interest, be considered."

"That it be dispensed with all Roman Catholic servants, male and female, for to live under the service of heretics, called Protestants, they swearing not to change their faith, or to become of their masters' or mistresses' religion; and to give their confessor notice whenever they shall hear any plot or matters against the Mother-Church or any of her clergy or members; also to help further and assist the cause of the Mother-Church whenever required by their Father Confessors.'

"That all Roman Catholic Counsels [counsellors] in the law pleading for heretics against Roman Catholics, are to give secret intelligence to some other party, if any flaw be in his heretical client's writings, that the said party may thereby inform the Roman Catholic, and the Counsel in the law not to be suspected, but supposed the Counsel of the Roman Catholic found it out by industry and learning in the law."

"That for encouraging all Roman Catholic servants to inform their Confessors with all matters that may prove prejudicial unto the Catholic cause, which may be practised or spoken by their heretical masters and mistresses, as they hear the same from time to time, to tell it to the Confessors; *so a pardon may be granted to such servants of all sins as oft as they inform their Confessors, and all penances taken off such, if any have been laid on them;* and in case the servant or servants be poor or needy, the Confessor to encourage the servant by giving some reward in money."

"*That all Roman Catholics taking the oath of allegiance unto any heretic king, prince or state, are to keep and observe* the same no longer than for the Mother-Church's advantage, or that there is urgent necessity; and so to dispense with any Roman Catholic as the Confessor shall see cause or reason; still the said Roman Catholic so taking the said oath, yet vowing and swearing to the Confessor he takes the oath of allegiance *in no other meaning or sense but to preserve himself from troubles, or for some temporal gain and profit,* and yet to succour the cause of the Mother-Church, as occasion shall serve, to the utmost of his power."

"That all Roman Catholics in offices, *dispensed with (for assuming any religion heretical),* do not speedily issue out writs, warrants, or attachments against any member of the Mother-Church, *without giving notice to the party, that the party might thereby escape, shun or avoid the same;* in so doing he shall testify his fidelity and obedience to the Roman faith and the Mother-Church."

"That all Roman Catholics in offices, thus dispensed with, if a judge, sheriff, bailiff, magistrate, or justice of the peace, shall have any member of the Mother-Church brought before them, they shall use their utmost to take off, qualify, or nullify the accusation judgment or impeachment, and take bail for that member, and take off the fine, in case the member so accused, indicted, or impeached, be in danger, and forced to escape for safety of his life, estate, &c.

"That all Roman Catholics thus dispensed with, if they shall be elected members of Parliament, they are not to give votes against Roman Catholics; or in case any heretical member shall start any proposal or question against the Mother-Church or her adherents, then to start some other question contrary to hinder the same, and to make underhand all friendship, as much as possibly can be, to oppose such proposals.

"That against the sittings of Parliaments in England a considerable sum of money be always in Bank, *ready to be disposed to several of the heretical members to befriend the Mother-Church's affairs;* and to be disposed of as the learned of the Roman Catholics so entrusted with the same shall think convenient.

"That the parties thus dispensed with, before their sitting in Parliament, be sworn by their Confessors to assure that they will labour all that in them lies to succour and support the Mother-Church's cause. *Then these said parties so dispensed with to receive their indulgences, and to be absolved from all oaths that are to be taken, or shall be taken, during the Session of Parliament.*

"That all Roman Catholics keeping taverns, inn-houses, ale or victualling-houses, so all Roman Catholics letting lodgings, shall discover to a holy Father of the Mother-Church all news, or whatever they shall hear, that is or may be prejudicial to the Mother-Church, or to her cause and affairs, within twenty-four hours at farthest, upon pain of an anathema or curse, or to their brother Catholic, to be related immediately without delay."

These licences, indulgences, and directions are stated to have been "copied out of a bundle of papers, sometime with the Most Rev. James Usher, Archbishop of Armagh, and supposed to be sent from beyond seas to him from the Rev. Bishop of Derry, afterwards his successor in Armagh [*i. e.,* John Bramhall], *being written with the same hand as the aforesaid letter was,* signed Jo. Derensis."*

Such were the instructions under which the agents of the Papacy acted in this country in the earlier part of the reign of Charles I. And no one who is able to estimate rightly the effects which a large body of unscrupulous agents of this kind can produce in any country, can be surprised at the state of moral confusion and disorder into which England was thrown at that period. And what added greatly to the magnitude of the evil was the secret admission of a Papal agent through the influence of the Queen and the tacit permission of the King, by whom the interests of the Papacy were in various ways promoted, and the chief persons, both in Church and State, tampered with and misled. A most remarkable and instructive account of the proceedings of this Romish agent, and their effects, is to be found in a work entitled, "The Memoirs of Gregorio Panzani, giving an account of his agency in Eng-

* Ibid. Pt. 3, pp. 175—188.

land in the years 1634, 1635, 1636," translated from the Italian original, and edited by the Rev. Joseph Berrington, Birmingham, 1793, 8vo.

A few extracts from these Memoirs will I think be found both interesting and instructive under the present circumstances of this country.

The agent selected by the Pope and Cardinal Barberini was Gregory Panzani, "a secular priest, of experienced virtue, of singular address, of polite learning, and in all respects well qualified for the business. The Queen was first made acquainted with the design, and she communicated it to the King, who gave his *tacit consent;* but at the same time *singular care was taken that the matter should not be divulged* among the Catholics or Protestants, who from different views might have obstructed its execution." (p. 132.)

Panzani at first acted with great caution, and did not "make himself known to either of the Secretaries of State," nor even to "the ambassadors of France and Spain" (p. 142); but in January 1635, he thought it time to "have an interview with Secretary Windebank;" Windebank being a "Protestant by profession, yet no enemy to the Catholics, and prepared to go all the lengths of the King and the Court party," and having "been made Secretary through the influence of Dr. Laud." (pp. 142, 160.) After this, "Panzani and Windebank had frequent opportunities of conferring together," and at last "they resolved that it should be proposed to the Queen and Cardinal Barberini, whether a mutual agency between the Court of Rome and England would not be very convenient." (p. 160.)

In the meantime, the presence of this Italian Papal agent in this country had been discovered by Cook, the other Secretary of State, a staunch Protestant, and of course, therefore, stigmatized in these Memoirs as "a Puritan;" and the Memoirs inform us, that "while Windebank and Panzani were carrying on their conferences, one Cook, a kind of Secretary, and by sect a Puritan, desired to have an audience of His Majesty," and "told His Majesty with a great deal of concern, that there was a certain Italian priest, named Panzani, sent secretly by the Pope, and who might be of dangerous consequence to the State, as well as to His Majesty's private affairs. The King smiled, telling the gentleman that he was no stranger to Panzani's arrival; that he was a person of worth and of unsuspected behaviour; that he had fully explained himself as to the reasons which brought him into England, and that he (Cook) *needed give himself no further trouble on that head.* The King however thought it proper, by the means of Windebank, to acquaint Panzani, that *though he was discovered by the Puritanical party, he might be easy;* that nobody should molest him." (pp. 153, 154.) And so the Royal victim left himself and his kingdom a prey to the subtle devices of the Papacy.

The next step, as might be expected, was an interview between Panzani and the King, in which compliments were mutually exchanged, the King assuring Panzani that "he had always received a very exalted idea of the merits of Urban VIII.," and Panzani replying that " he knew it to be His Holiness's desire that the Catholics should be punctual in their obedience to His Majesty." (pp. 161, 162.)

"This interview," it is added, " encouraged Windebank to treat more familiarly with Panzani, especially on the head of religion. He told him that he really looked on himself to be a good Catholic; otherwise that he should make no difficulty to bid adieu to all that was dear to him in order to purchase that name." And he remarked, " If we had neither Jesuits nor Puritans in England, I am confident an union might easily be effected." He " afterwards proceeded further in his discourse concerning an union, assuring Panzani that *all the moderate men in Church and State thirsted after it.*" And Panzani suggested that, while the terms were being agreed upon, " *a decree for liberty of conscience would be a good expedient.*" (pp. 162—164.)

" Father Philip, the Queen's Confessor, had incidentally some discourse with the King on matters of the same tendency, in which he endeavoured to persuade His Majesty, that it was directly opposite to the whole design of the Gospel, that there should be *more Churches than one;* whence he inferred *the necessity of a re-union."* (p. 165.)

While these conferences were going on, a Mr. Davenport, a Franciscan friar, otherwise called *Franciscus a Sancta Clara*, published the work which has lately been again brought so much under the notice of the public, entitled, " Deus, Natura, Gratia," in which an attempt is made to reconcile the Thirty-nine Articles with the decrees of the Council of Trent. " This book," it is said, " was highly esteemed by His Majesty, as being full of complaisance for the Protestant systems in several points, ... but the work was far from being liked at the Roman Court, where it was considered as a very dangerous production, far too condescending to schismatics and heretics." (p. 165.)

The great object Panzani and Windebank had first in view was, to establish "a reciprocal agency" between the Court of Rome and the Queen of England, *"the design of which was to make an experiment, how far the two Churches could be brought towards a union."* And Father Philip, the Queen's Confessor, " a person of great penetration, who had made it his business ever since he came into England to observe the religious dispositions of the nation," sent Cardinal Barberini the following account—an account the moral aspect of which is well worth consideration at the present day :—
" That the King and several of his Ministry were far from being adverse to an union : that it was an undertaking of the most dangerous consequence, on account of the many and severe edicts that were in force against the Roman Catholic religion : that those who were *most favourably inclined to the Catholic cause* were frequently obliged to give proofs of *their zeal to the contrary for fear* of notice ; in which case it was difficult to form a just idea of their real sentiments, seeing they found themselves under a necessity of *varying from themselves* and *acting incoherently.* For instance, he said, when there was any pressing occasion for money, the King was obliged, contrary to his inclination, to

let the laws loose against the Roman Catholics, otherwise the Puritanical House of Commons would make no progress in the money bills; for the Government not being arbitrary, no extraordinary levies would be granted without the people's consent. That *the bishops in like manner (though several of them were disposed to enter into a correspondence with Rome) when their temporalities were threatened by the Puritanical members (as they had frequently been of late), went into the same persecuting methods;* that such a conduct as this had so much of contradiction in it, that it was *altogether unintelligible to those who were not perfectly acquainted with the infirmities of human nature,* and particularly with the irresolution of these islanders. Yet, after all, if Windebank's project of a reciprocal agency could be set on foot, there might be some hopes of a re-union." "Then," it is added, "Father Philip goes on and acquaints the Cardinal with the qualities of the agents proper to engage on such an undertaking; particularly he gives his opinion of the Italian agent," who is to be about 35 years of age, "noble, rich, handsome, and affable in conversation," "grave and reserved, yet complaisant, *especially to the ladies of the Court,* and still here very guarded," and skilful in various ways; and "everyone" is to be "accosted in their own way and *enticed by proper baits.*" "Then," it continues, "he proceeds to give his opinion how things ought to be managed, after the goodwill of the Ministry and Privy Council shall have been secured, viz., 'That none of the laws against Roman Catholics be executed, without an express and written order from above to every inferior office, *which will afford time to ward off the blow,* and amount to an interpretative liberty of conscience, and at the same time be an encouragement to moderate Protestants to speak their minds freely in favour of Roman Catholics. This might be followed afterwards by *more particular allowances for liberty of conscience, and so on gradually, till it became general;* and then *in a few years the leading men of both Houses might be induced to think of an union.*" (pp. 186—189.)

"After frequent consultations, the King was pleased to name Robert Douglas to be the agent on the Queen's part," but on his death shortly after, the King appointed a Mr. Arthur Brett. "The king in this affair was entirely under the direction of the Queen; yet he enjoined the party to be *cautious and secret, for should such a correspondence, he observed, once get wind, it would be highly resented by the generality of the nation.*" (pp. 197—200.) It was, in fact, illegal.

The account of Mr. Brett's mission was received with peculiar pleasure at Rome, and the Pope took steps for appointing an agent on his part to send to England; but through Mr. Brett's death, the matter was again delayed, and ultimately a Mr. Hamilton was appointed the agent from England to the Pope, and Mr. George Conn, a Scotchman, who had been resident some time in Rome, was sent by the Pope to England. (p. 233.)

But before Mr. Conn's arrival the project of a union between the Churches of Rome and England got wind, and drew out an expression of the feelings of those to whom such a scheme was attractive. And these Memoirs of Panzani show *how much may be going on under the surface in a matter of this kind, of which the public mind is altogether ignorant.* "The persons employed," it is said, "were often enjoined secrecy," (p. 237,) but too many knew the secret to allow of its being kept. And the following account will I think be read with interest in the present day:—

"Among those that most suspected these proceedings was Montague, bishop of Chichester, a person of remarkable learning and *moderation*. This gentleman's curiosity led him so far as to desire a private interview with Panzani. When they met, he immediately fell upon the project of an union, as if he had been already acquainted with the whole affair. He signified a great desire that the breach between the two churches might be made up, and apprehended no danger from publishing the scheme, as things now stood. He said he had frequently made it the subject of his most serious thoughts, and had diligently considered all the requisites of an union; adding that he was satisfied both the Archbishops, with the Bishop of London and several others of the Episcopal order, besides a great number of the learned inferior clergy, were prepared to fall in with the Church of Rome as to a supremacy purely spiritual; and that there was no other method of ending controversies, than by having recourse to some centre of ecclesiastical unity. . . . . . . [Adding much more in the same strain, though, no doubt, Panzani's account of the matter is such as is the most favourable to Rome.] . . . . Bishop Montague . . . . told him at parting that he would take the first opportunity to discourse the Primate on the subject, but insinuated that he was a *cautious man*, who would make no advances unless he were *well protected.*"

" This conference between Bishop Montague and Panzani being transmitted to Rome, the Italians were extremely pleased with it. . . . . . . Panzani in return was ordered to acquaint the bishop, what a value they had for him at Rome, and how much his learning and pacific dispositions were applauded, with an exhortation that he *would continue the good work he had begun, and never cease till* he had brought that distracted nation back and directed them into the paths of their ancestors. As for looking into particular controversies, or specifying the terms of communion, it was too soon to speak on those matters. *At present* it would be most advisable to dwell upon *generals:* and especially the Protestant bishops and clergy ought to examine the motives which first occasioned the breach with Rome, which being found human and unwarrantable, it would be their duty to come forward and *sue for a reconciliation.* Afterwards particular points might be debated with some hopes of an accommodation, *when there was a Court of Judicature established to pronounce upon them.* They might assure themselves, the Bishop of Rome would make no unreasonable demands, but content himself with the essentials of his primacy, and such privileges as were annexed to it *jure divino.*

" Panzani is then directed by the Cardinal to inquire into

the characters of the Protestant bishops; for as they were to be employed in the projected scheme of union, it was requisite to be fully informed what sort of men they were, and how qualified as to learning, morals, religion, politics, &c., that those who were to treat with them might know *how to come at them by proper and suitable addresses*. But he had a strict charge to be *very cautious and secret in the inquiry*. Above all things Panzani was advised never to favour the discussion of particular points, the issue of such conferences being always fruitless. Besides, it was never the custom of the Catholic Church to admit of such kind of disputes, *till the fundamental point of a supreme judge were first settled, for then other matters would come in of course.* . . . . In a word, authority and doctrinal points were the two capital objects; and *the first was to be determined before the other could be debated.**

"Having received these instructions from Rome, Panzani took the first opportunity to wait on Bishop Montague. He omitted not to acquaint him how much he was admired in Italy on account of the many and excellent qualifications he was master of. The bishop, who was not a little vain, relished the compliment, and returned it, as far as was convenient, upon his admirers. He repeated his former discourse concerning the union, adding that he was *continually employed in disposing men's minds for it, both by words and writing*, as often as he met with an opportunity. He then again mentioned the Pope's supremacy, whose feet he said he was willing to kiss, and acknowledge himself to be one of his children. He added that *the Archbishop of Canterbury was entirely of his sentiment, but with a great allay of fear and caution*. Then he renewed the proposal of appointing deputies on both sides.

"Panzani replied, that he had orders not to touch upon particulars, nor give encouragement that there should be

---

* The reader will observe how *subjection to the Bishop of Rome* is the prime fundamental; and of course, when this is yielded, complete mental slavery follows.

any relaxation on the Catholic side as to the *credenda* or fundamentals of religion, observing that the union designed was not only to be politic and ceremonial, but real and *in unitate fidei*, without any mixture of creeds. The bishop assured him that he aimed at a total union.

"The truth is, Panzani was apprehensive the bishop still entertained some opinions inconsistent with the fundamentals of the Roman Catholic religion. . . . . .

"From the whole it was pretty plain that there was a great inclination in many of the eminent Protestant clergy to re-unite themselves to the see of Rome: but they kept themselves to themselves, never imparting their minds to one another, much less to the king, for they imagined the spiritual supremacy was a prerogative he would not easily part with. . . . . Of the sentiments the great men of those times had of the matter, there was one instance. Dr. George Leyburn assured Panzani, *in verbo sacerdotis*, that the Archbishop of Canterbury encouraged the Duchess of Buckingham to remain contented, for in a little time she would see England re-united to the See of Rome.*

. . . .

"It was not long before there was another interview between Panzani and the Bishop of Chichester. . . . Panzani being curious to know the characters of the chief of the Protestant clergy, Montague told him, there were only three bishops that could be counted violently bent against the Church of Rome, viz., Durham, Salisbury, and Exeter, (Morton, Davenant, and Hall); the rest he said were *very moderate*. But *Panzani received a particular character of each bishop from another hand. It gave an account of their age, family, way of life, qualifications, natural and acquired, moral and political, and, as far as could be guessed, how they stood affected as to the present management of affairs at Court. This account was carefully transmitted to Barberini.* . . . . .
. . . . . . Panzani once more falling on the union, expressed

---

* These statements may not all be quite exact, but they illustrate the state of things at this period, and show the tendency of certain minds.

himself in a very desponding manner, considering the many difficulties with which they had to struggle. 'Well,' said the bishop, 'had you been acquainted with this nation ten years ago, you might have observed such an alteration in the language and inclinations of the people, that it would not only put you in hopes of an union, but you would conclude it was near at hand.' Then he solemnly declared, that both he and many of his brethren were prepared to conform themselves to the method and discipline of the Gallican Church, where the civil rights were well guarded; *and as for the aversion we discover in our sermons and printed books, they are things of form, chiefly to humour the populace, and not to be much regarded.*'"

"Among those of the Episcopal order who seemed to desire an union, none appeared more zealous than Dr. Goodman, of Gloucester, who every day said the Priest's office, and observed several other duties as practised in the Church of Rome."* (pp. 237—249.)

"Soon after the arrival of Mr. Conn at London, Panzani was recalled," and took leave of the king and queen, &c., "nor did he omit to pay his respects to some of the ladies of distinction about Court, who, though Protestants, recommended themselves to his Holiness, and desired his blessing. It was the end of the year 1636." On his return to Rome, Panzani was rewarded with a rich canonry, and afterwards made bishop of Mileto. (pp. 255—257.)

From these extracts, the reader will be able to judge of the nature and effects of Panzani's agency in this country, and the extent to which the designs of Rome were promoted by it. His mission was a dexterous expedient of the Court of Rome, under the especial guidance of Cardinal Barberini, to cajole and allure the leading men in Church and State to recognize the supremacy of the Pope, and facilitate the reunion of the two Churches; while at the same time (in the apprehen-

---

* Dr. Goodman afterwards joined the Church of Rome, and died in its Communion in 1655. The above statements, with every allowance for some exaggeration, show what was going on in our Church at that period, and read an instructive lesson to us at the present time.

sion, probably, of the failure of this scheme) the more unscrupulous agents, sent over chiefly though not solely by the Jesuits, threw the whole kingdom into confusion by breaking it up into parties, political and ecclesiastical, bitterly hostile to each other. And we shall find that when the hope of gaining over the king and a sufficient number of the leading men in Church and State to the Papal cause had ceased, the Jesuit agents redoubled their efforts, and the Papal Nuncio that succeeded Panzani was leagued with them in their criminal attempts to involve a "heretical" king, nation, and Church in a chaos of confusion, out of which they might rise triumphant as the restorers of peace and order to a people torn with internal dissensions.

Of the credit due to the work from which I have quoted, there can be no reasonable doubt. Mr. Berrington has appended to the "Memoirs," "Remarks subjoined to the M.S. copy of the Memoirs, by Mr. Dodd," who says,—"If the author was not Panzani himself, he certainly was some other who had his Memoirs and private notes in keeping. The original is in Italian, from which it was translated by an eminent prelate of singular candour and scrupulosity." And to the possible objection of his co-religionists to its being published, that "it exposes too much the intrigues of the Court of Rome against the Church of England," he candidly replies, that "the whole affair of the English Mission may be called an intrigue against the Established Church, if we regard the end and purposes of it; and of this we may be informed without Panzani's Memoirs." (pp. 258—261.)

How far the inclination to favour Popery, and support the scheme of a reunion between the two Churches, actually extended among the leading men of that time, it is impossible now to determine. But there can, I think, be no doubt, that the *virus* of Popery had deeply affected many of them, and that circumstances alone, and more particularly *the strong Protestant feeling of the great majority of the nation*, prevented their inclination towards Popery from issuing in some direct efforts in its behalf.

The account given in Panzani's Memoirs receives considerable confirmation from the statements of a tract published in 1643, intitled "The Pope's Nuncioes," "affirmed," as Heylin tells us, "to have been written by a Venetian ambassador at his being in England," (and therefore, it must be recollected, a Romish representation of the matter,) from which Heylin gives some extracts, including the following; which, however, I quote from the original:—

"As to a reconciliation between the Churches of England and Rome there were made some general propositions and overtures by the Archbishop's agents, they assuring that his Grace was very much disposed thereunto ; and that if it was not accomplished in his lifetime, it would prove a work of more difficulty after his death : that in very truth for the last three years the Archbishop had introduced some innovations approaching the rites and forms of Rome ; that the Bishop of Chichester [Montague], a great confident of his Grace, and the Lord Treasurer, and eight other Bishops of his Grace's party, did most passionately desire a reconciliation with the Church of Rome ; that they did day by day recede from their ancient tenets to accommodate with the Church of Rome; that therefore the Pope on his part ought to make some steps to meet them, and the Court of Rome remit something of its rigour in doctrine, otherwise no accord could be. And in very deed the Universities, bishops, and divines of this realm do daily embrace Catholic opinions, though they *profess not so much with open mouth for fear of the Puritans*..... In sum, that they believe all that is taught by the Church, but not by the Court of Rome."*
"Both the Archbishop and Bishop of Chichester have said often, that there are but two sorts of persons likely to impeach and hinder reconciliation, to wit, Puritans amongst the Protestants and Jesuits amongst the Catholics."†

And so far is Dr. Heylin, the friend of Laud and Chaplain to Charles I., from denying the truth of this representation, that he quotes the passage as to the Universities, &c. "em-

* The Pope's Nuncioes. London, 1643, 4to, pp. 11, 12. † Ib. p. 16.

bracing Catholic opinions," as showing "how far they had proceeded towards this HAPPY *reconciliation.*"*

The two Secretaries, Windebank and Cottington, and Dr. Goodman, Bishop of Gloucester, afterwards openly joined the Church of Rome. The King and Archbishop Laud allowed themselves to be drawn some way towards it, but on a nearer view shrank from committing themselves altogether to it, their consciences unwillingly detecting some points to which they *feared* to give approval.

That Archbishop Laud looked favourably upon the project of a reconciliation with Rome, and acted in many respects with an eye to the promotion of it, (though, it is to be hoped, with a considerable reserve in the extent to which his concessions would have gone,) can hardly be doubted even from the statements of his friend Heylin himself. Dr. Heylin, referring to a tract called "The English Pope," printed at London in the same year 1643, says—"*He* WELL TELLS US *that after Con had undertook the managing of the affairs, matters began to grow toward some agreement;*" and then stating what it was supposed the Pope was likely to yield, he adds,—"*And to obtain a reconciliation upon these advantages the Archbishop had all the reason in the world* TO DO AS HE DID *in ordering the Lord's table to be placed where the Altar stood, and making the accustomed reverence in all approaches towards it and accesses to it; in beautifying and adorning churches, and celebrating the Divine service with all due solemnities; in taking care that all offensive and exasperating passages should be expunged out of such books as were brought to the press and for reducing the extravagancy of some opinions to an evener temper* . . . . . and if he approved *auricular confession,* and showed himself willing to introduce it into the use of the Church, as both our authors say he did, it is no more than what the Liturgy commends to the care of the penitent (though we find not the word 'auricular' in it), or what the Canons have provided for in the point of security for such as shall be willing to confess themselves."†

* See Heylin's Life of Laud, bk. 4, under year 1639.　　† Ibid.

Such is the statement of Heylin himself.

But when, after raising the expectations of the Romanists, the King and Archbishop, impelled probably by *various motives*, impeded their proceedings, they became doubly the objects of their hatred, especially with the Jesuits; to whose views, indeed, however much they might be inclined towards effecting, if possible, a union with the Church of Rome, they were probably to a great extent opposed. And the object of the Jesuits being, as expressed in one of the documents already quoted, to bring about a "*universal catholic monarchy*"—*an object which to this day they have more at heart than any other*—they were as anxious to get rid of those who, while they approximated to them in some points, opposed their main scheme, as of more thorough opponents.

And I now proceed to show how the designs of Rome were carried on by the successor of Panzani.

Of this we have indisputable evidence in some documents found among Archbishop Laud's papers. They consist of letters written by Sir W. Boswell, King Charles the First's agent at the Hague, enclosing statements made by one who had been in the confidence of the Romanists, but left them in disgust,* of the secret plots and conspiracies of the Romanists against both the King and Archbishop Laud. These letters and statements had all of them the Archbishop's own endorsement as to the party from whom they came and the time when they were received, and among them was a letter from the Archbishop to the King, calling his serious attention to the matter, which had been returned to the Archbishop with the King's notes on it in his own handwriting in the margin.

The last statement, of the date of Oct., 1640, contains a full discovery of the practices and objects of these Romish agents, from which I give the following extracts.

Premising that "all those Factions with which all Christendom was at that day shaken" arose from the Jesuits, it states that they are divided into "Four Orders," which

---

* The name *assumed* was, Andrew Habernfeld; but it is clear that this was only an assumed name.

"abound throughout the world," and thus proceeds,—" Of the *first* Order are ecclesiastics, whose office is to take care of things promoting religion. Of the *second* Order are politicians, whose office it is by any means to *shake, trouble, reform* the state of kingdoms and republics. Of the *third* Order are Seculars, whose property it is to obtrude themselves into offices with kings and princes, to insinuate and immix themselves in Court-businesses, bargains and sales, and to be busied in civil affairs. Of the *fourth* Order are Intelligencers (or Spies), men of inferior condition who submit themselves to the services of great men, princes, barons, noblemen, citizens, to deceive (or corrupt) the minds of their masters.

"A Society of so many Orders the Kingdom of England nourisheth; for scarce all Spain, France, and Italy can yield so great a multitude of Jesuits as London alone, where are found more than fifty Scottish Jesuits;* there the said Society hath elected to itself a seat of iniquity, and hath conspired against the King, and the most faithful to the King, especially the Lord Bishop of Canterbury, and likewise against both kingdoms.

"For it is more certain than certainty itself that the forenamed Society hath *determined to effect an universal Reformation of the Kingdom of England and Scotland.* . . . .

"Therefore to promote the undertaken villainy, the said Society dubbed itself with the title of '*The congregation of propagating the faith*,'† which acknowledgeth the Pope of Rome the Head of the College, and Cardinal Barberini his substitute and executor.

"The chief Patron of the Society at London is the Pope's Legate, who takes care of the business; into whose bosom these dregs of traitors weekly deposit all their intelligences. Now the residence of this Legation was obtained at London in the name of the Roman Pontiff, by whose mediation it might be lawful for Cardinal Barberini to work so much the more easily and safely upon the King and Kingdom; for

* The reader will observe to what extent the efforts of these secret agents may be carried on while the public mind is utterly unconscious of them.

† The reader will observe here the origin and special object of this Society.

none else could so freely circumvent the King, as he who should be palliated with the Pope's authority.

"*Master Cuneus did at that time enjoy the office of the Pope's Legate*, an universal instrument of the conjured Society, and a serious promoter of the business, whose secrets, as likewise those of all the other intelligencers, the present good man, the communicator of all these things, did receive and expedite whither the business required.

"Cuneus set upon the chief men of the kingdom, and left nothing unattempted by what means he might corrupt them all, and incline them to the Pontifical Party. He enticed many with various incitements, yea, he sought to delude the King himself with gifts of pictures, antiquities, idols, and of other vanities brought from Rome. . . . . . .

"In the meantime, Cuneus smelling from the Archbishop most trusty to the King, that the King's mind was wholly pendulous (or doubtful), resolved, that he would move every stone and apply his forces, that he might gain him to his party, certainly confiding that he had a means prepared, for he had a command to offer a Cardinal's cap to the Lord Archbishop in the name of the Pope of Rome.* . . . .

"Another also was assayed, Secretary Cook, who hindered access to the detestable wickedness. . . . . Hereupon being made odious to the Patrons of the conspiracy, he was endangered to be discharged from his office; *it was laboured for about three years and at last obtained*. . . . . . .

"When Cuneus had understood from the Lord Archbishop's party, that he had laboured in vain, his malice and the whole Society's waxed boiling hot. Soon after ambushes began to be prepared, *wherewith the Lord Archbishop, together with the King, should be taken*. . . . . .

* It appears from the Archbishop's own Diary that this offer had been made to him before, as it is there stated by himself:—"Aug. 4, 1633. At Greenwich there came one to me seriously, and that avowed ability to perform it, and offered me to be a Cardinal;" and again, "Aug. 17. Saturday. I had a serious offer made me again to be a Cardinal;" and he himself states that his answer was as follows,—"My answer again was, THAT SOMEWHAT DWELT WITHIN ME, *which would not suffer that, till Rome were otherwise than it is.*" No wonder that, with such an answer, Rome still entertained, for some time after, the hope of his reconciliation to her communion.

"In this heat a certain Scottish Earl, called Maxfeld, if I mistake not, was expedited to the Scots by the Popish party, with whom two other Scottish Earls, Papists, held correspondency. He ought [? sought] to stir up the people to commotion, and rub over the injury afresh, that he might inflame their minds, precipitate them to arms, by which the hurtful disturber of the Scottish liberty might be slain.

"There, by one labour, snares are prepared for the King; for this purpose the present business was so ordered, that very many of the English should adhere to the Scots; that the King should remain inferior in arms, who (thereupon) should be compelled to crave assistance from the Papists; which yet he should not obtain, unless he would descend into conditions, by which he should permit universal liberty of exercise of the Popish Religion; for so the affairs of the Papists would succeed according to their desire. To which consent if he should show himself more difficult, there should be a present remedy at hand; for the King's son growing now very fast to his youthful age, (*who is educated from his tender age that he might accustom himself to the Popish party,*) the King is to be *despatched;* for an Indian nut stuffed with most sharp poison is kept in the Society (which Cuneus* at that time *showed often to me* in a boasting manner) wherein a poison was prepared for the King, after the example of his Father.†

"In this Scottish commotion the Marquis of Hamilton, often despatched to the Scots in the name of the King, to interpose the Royal authority, whereby the heat of minds might be mitigated, *returned notwithstanding as often without fruit, and without ending the business.* HIS CHAPLAIN AT THAT TIME REPAIRED TO US, WHO COMMUNICATED SOME THINGS SECRETLY WITH CUNEUS.‡

. . . .

* The Pope's Nuncio, Con.
† A confirmation of the rumours that got abroad at the time, of the mode in which James I. met his death.
‡ The reader will observe here how the most important political interests of the kingdom suffered from the unfaithfulness of a Popish agent under the disguise of a Protestant clergyman.

"Sir Toby Matthew, a Jesuited priest, of the Order of Politicians, a most vigilant man of the chief heads . . . . . flies to all banquets and feasts, called or not called, never quiet, always in action and perpetual motion. Thrusting himself into all conversation of superiors, he urgeth conferences familiarly, that he may fish out the minds of men. Whatever he observeth thence which may bring any commodity or discommodity to the part of the conspirators, he communicates to the Pope's Legate; the more secret things he himself writes to the Pope or to Cardinal Barberini. In sum, he adjoins himself to any man's company; no word can be spoken, that he will not lay hold on, and accommodate to his Party. In the meantime, whatever he hath fished out, he reduceth into a catalogue, and every summer carrieth it to the general Consistory of the Jesuits Politicks, which secretly meet together in the Province of Wales, where he is an acceptable guest. *There counsels are secretly hammered, which are most meet for the convulsion of the ecclesiastic and politic estate of both kingdoms.*

"Captain Read, a Scot, dwelling in Long-acre Street, near the Angel Tavern, a Secular Jesuit, who for his detestable office performed (whereby he had perverted a certain minister of the Church, with secret incitements, to the Popish religion, with all his family, taking his daughter to wife) for a recompense obtained a rent or impost upon butter, which the country people are bound to render to him, *procured for him from the King by some chief men of the Society*, who never want a spur, whereby he may be constantly detained in his office. In his house the business of the whole plot is concluded, where the Society which hath conspired against the King, the Lord Archbishop, and both kingdoms, meet together for the most part every day. But on the day of the Carrier's (or Post's) despatch, which is ordinarily Friday, they meet in greater numbers; for then all the Intelligencers assemble and confer in common, what things every of them hath fished out that week; who that they may be without suspicion, send their secrets by Toby Matthew, or

Read himself, to the Pope's Legate; he transmits the compacted pacquet, which he hath purchased from the Intelligencers, to Rome. With the same Read the letters brought from Rome are deposited, under feigned titles and names, who [which] by him are delivered to all to whom they appertain, for all and every of their names are known to him. Upon the very same occasion letters also are brought hither under the covert of Father Philip, (he notwithstanding being ignorant of things,) from whom they are distributed to the conspirators. . . . .

"Those who assemble in the fore-named house come frequently in coaches, or on horseback in laymen's habit, and with a great train, wherewith they are disguised, that they may not be known; yet they are Jesuits and conjured members of the Society.

"All the Papists of England contribute to this assembly, lest anything should be wanting to promote the undertaken design. . . . .

"Besides the foresaid houses, there are conventicles also kept at other more secret places, of which verily they confide not even among themselves, for fear lest they should be discovered. First every of them are called to certain Inns, (one not knowing of the other); hence they are severally led by spies to the place where they ought to meet, otherwise ignorant where they ought to assemble, lest peradventure they should be surprised at unawares.

"The Countess of Arundel, a strenuous she-champion of the Popish religion, binds all her nerves to the Universal Reformation; whatsoever she hears at the King's Court, that is done secretly or openly in words or deeds, she presently imparts to the Pope's Legate, with whom she meets thrice a day.

. . . .

"Master Porter of the King's bedchamber, most addicted to the Popish religion, is a bitter enemy of the King; *he reveals all his greatest secrets to the Pope's Legate;* although he very rarely meets with him, yet *his wife meets him so much the oftener;* who being informed by her husband, conveys secrets to the Legate. In all his actions he is nothing inferior to Toby Matthew; it cannot be uttered how diligently he watcheth on the business. *His sons are secretly instructed in the Romish religion; openly they profess the Reformed.* The eldest is now to receive his father's office *under the King which shall be;* a Cardinal's hat is provided for the other, if the design shall succeed well.

. . . .

" Secretary Windebanke, a most fierce Papist, is the most unfaithful to the King of all men; who not only betrays and reveals even the King's secrets, but likewise communicates counsels by which the design may be best advanced. He at least thrice every week converseth with the Legate in nocturnal conventicles, and reveals those things which he thinks fit to be known; for which end he hired a house near to the Legate's house, whom he often resorts to through the garden door; for by this vicinity the meeting is facilitated.* . . . . .

" Sir Digby, Sir Winter, Master Mountague the younger, who hath been at Rome, my Lord Sterling, a cousin of the Earl of Arundel's, a Knight, the Countess of Newport, the Duchess of Buckingham, and many others who have sworn into this conspiracy, are all most vigilant in the design. Some of these are enticed with the hope of Court, others of Political, offices; others attend to the sixteen Cardinal's caps that are vacant; which are therefore detained idle for some years, that they may impose a vain hope on those who expect them.

. . . .

" The Pope's Legate useth a threefold character or cypher; one, wherewith he communicates with the Nuncios; another with Cardinal Barberini only; a third, wherewith he covers some greater secrets to be communicated."

This statement had " the Archbishop's indorsement with his own hand. Rec. Octob. 14, 1640."†

* In the December after this discovery, on a peremptory summons to appear before the House of Commons, he fled beyond sea, and soon openly joined the Church of Rome.
† Rome's Master-piece. London: 1643. 4to; and from it in Foxes and Firebrands, Pt. 3, pp. 92—141, and Rushworth's Historical Collections,

It may seem surprising that more notice was not taken of this secret information by the King and Archbishop, who, on the receipt of the first letter from Sir W. Boswell, evidently took a serious view of the matter, as appears from the Archbishop's letter to the King, and the King's notes upon it, alluded to above. But in Heylin's Life of Laud we find the explanation in a passage showing *with what consummate duplicity some of the principal actors in the plot had played their parts;* a duplicity which events had evidently led Heylin to suspect even at the time he wrote, but which subsequent revelations, especially in Panzani's Memoirs, have fully brought to light.

On the receipt of the first letter from Sir W. Boswell, Heylin tells us,—" So far both the King and he had very good reason to be sensible of the dangers which were threatened to them. But when the large discovery was brought unto him transmitted in Boswell's letter of the 15th of October, *he found some names in it which discredited the whole relation as well in his Majesty's judgment as his own.* For besides his naming of some profest Papists . . . . of whose fidelity the King was not willing to have any suspicion, he named the Earl of Arundel, Windebank, principal Secretary of State, and Porter, one of the Grooms of the Bedchamber, whom he charged to be the King's utter enemies, and such as betrayed his secrets to the Pope's Nuncio upon all occasions; *all which his Majesty beheld as men of most approved loyalty and affections to him;* by reason whereof *no further credit being given to the advertisement* which they had from Boswell, the danger so much feared at first be-

Pt. ii. vol. 2, pp. 1310—1323. It is also quoted by Heylin in his Life of Laud, anno 1639, and again 1640. All the documents connected with this matter were first published by order of a Committee of the House of Commons, by W. Prynne (who found them among the Archbishop's Papers), in the tract above referred to, entitled "Rome's Master-piece." Habernfield's letters are in Latin, and the original Latin is given by Prynne, together with the translation which is cited above. The remark of the Archbishop in his endorsement on the first letter is,—" I conceive by the English Latin herein, that he must needs be an Englishman with a concealed and changed name. And yet it may be this kind of Latin may relate to the Italian. Or else he lived some good time in England."

came more slighted and neglected than consisted with his Majesty's safety, and the condition of the times, which were apt to mischief. For though the party who first broke the ice to this intelligence might be mistaken in the names of some of the accomplices . . . . *yet the calamities which soon after fell upon them both, the deplorable death of the Archbishop first and his Majesty afterwards, declare sufficiently, that there was some greater reality in the plot than the King was willing to believe.*"*

Subsequent revelations, through the publication of Panzani's Memoirs and other sources of information, have shown that there was no such "mistake," and that the professed Protestantism and " approved loyalty and affection" of these supposed friends were only the masks assumed by agents of Rome the more effectually to carry on their designs, and which rendered them far more dangerous than open Papists. In fact, it appears from this statement of Dr. Heylin, that the neglect with which this discovery of the plot was treated was entirely due to the way in which the duplicity of these parties had blinded the eyes of the King and Archbishop to their real character and proceedings.

In the meantime the conspirators proceeded gradually and carefully but surely to the accomplishment of their schemes, and the following letter, written from London, May 13, 1642, from a Jesuit agent, using the name of J. Fagan, to " the Sacred and Holy Society of Jesus at Paris," which came into the hands of Archbishop Usher in 1652, (several copies of which he gave to his friends,) will show the nature of the course they pursued.

" Reverend Sirs,—We doubt not but to make a great progress in what we have undertaken; we have put the *Mobile* out of conceit with Canterbury, the head of their heretical Episcopacy, and doubt not in time to perfect our designs *through fractions between themselves. It must not be totally arms that can conquer heresy, as you have advised, but* SEPARATION, *which hath prevailed much of late.* Many of

* Heylin's Life of Laud, lib. v., under the year 1640.

the common sort are fallen from the heretic bishops, and are for a synod or assembly of presbyters, who shall soon eclipse their pomp. *We be encouraging the Independents purposely to balance the scales, lest they grow too ponderous, high, and lofty. And as we shall find them also, we shall encourage the Anabaptists, knowing all these are a distraction to a heretical monarchy.* ..... We shall hinder the heretics by finding them work at home, and thereby prevent their sending aid for Ireland; for *we have parties of great skill and policy* ON BOTH SIDES, *as well with the Parliament crew as with the King;* so that if either take, we are safe, so we do not discover our projects to our adversaries. We intreat you to signify unto the Convent, that we want wise, learned, and subtle scholars to come and *assist these new sects, that they may still be at variance,* especially amongst the Parliamentaries; and for the other party with the King, we have equality, and fear them not. The old cub Canterbury suspects not the Church Catholic in the least, but is inveterate against the Puritan sort, and they against him; which is a just judgment on him for his inveterate piece written against Father Fisher. We seem *very civil to him,* and *cherish him against the Puritans,* whilst we visit him; so that HE DREAMS NOT HOW THE NET IS SPREAD TO CATCH HIM.

"Consider of these things, and consult the Cardinal with them. Let a supply of money be sent for. We must encourage the undertakers, and bribe others, otherwise it may not only prolong but oppose causes. ...... In the meantime acknowledging the authority of the Superior and power of the Holy Society, I conclude always their true and faithful slave and obedient member to advance the cause of the holy Catholic and Mother-Church of Rome till death, J. FAGAN."*

The reader will observe that this letter was written just at the commencement of the civil war, and after Laud had been committed to the Tower. And it is clear from it that the object of the party was to gain their ends partly by "arms," but more especially by the "separation" of the nation into

* Foxes and Firebrands, Pt. 3, pp. 150—153.

antagonistic parties, and that they had cunningly managed to introduce "parties of great skill and policy on both sides, as well with the Parliament crew as with the King," so as to prevent reconciliation between them, and at the same time secure their own ends, whichever side might prevail; and that they were secretly working for the downfall of Archbishop Laud, as one who, with all his leanings towards a modified Popery, stood in the way of the accomplishment of their schemes.

Such is the way in which the Church of Rome labours for the promotion of the religion of Jesus Christ!

And it is remarkable how little practical effect even the publication by the House of Commons, in 1643, of the documents above quoted, found among Archbishop Laud's papers, seems to have had; though, as was pointed out at the time by their editor, the course of events had been such as strongly to confirm the truth of the revelations there made.

One more revelation of the workings of this "mystery of iniquity" is afforded us by another letter from the same party, a copy of which came at the same time (1652) into the hands of Archbishop Usher. It is dated London, April 6, 1645, three years after the former, and when Presbyterianism had risen on the ruins of Episcopacy, and the Scottish army, among whom probably were the "northern correspondents" referred to in the letter, had gained considerable power, and not long before the King adopted the extraordinary and fatal step of taking shelter in that army.

"Reverend Fathers,—We and our brethren (as our brother in Jesu can inform you) have with all diligence and art (as much as nature can afford or human reason endow us) perfected [fulfilled] the ordinances and statutes of the Holy Society; our adversaries the heretics being neither the wiser, nor mistrusting our order or function in the least; so that our drifts will take, if continued as is begun; they still in anywise not mistrusting our Catholic intentions. *Be ye not dismayed nor jealous of our Northern correspondents. Although they term you sons of the Whore of Babylon, at present we cannot help it.* Yet we term the Episcopacy of the heretical tribe of this nation the same, purposely for our proper ends and assurance of perfecting a toleration for consciences.

"We desire some able assistance from you and other places; as from Italy, Portugal, and Spain; and also your counsel and theirs, especially whilst this heretical synod of presbyters rule and govern; truly we find them a perverse sort of heretics to clash with; for since they have become masters, and conquered the heretical bishops, we find great opposition and require more assistance.

"It is not ripe enough as yet to set Anabaptism a-madding at this time, but rather *set enmity and variance between Sir John Presbyter* (that tribe of John Calvin their Master) *and the Independant.* Jesu Mary be praised, that tribe holds Sir John tug. We have sent private intelligence unto *Patience*,* hearing he and that tribe have lately fallen out in New England, encouraging [him] to return; for here he may better clash with a Presbyterian than with those, being bred up and trained up for that sect, and there be less suspected.

"I here send you a roll of the names who contend with Sir John's tribe. . . . . As for the rest of their names, how they be qualified, what points they stand upon, and *what new doctrines they have spread,* the roll will inform the Society.

"The Anabaptists increase a-main; and Peter Pain, who was lately discovered, hath fled from these parts, and is gone into Yorkshire, where he goeth now under the name of T. C. *Look into the Licence book, and you will know under what names he was to go in case of discovery.*

"I suppose the Deputy-Provincial hath given you all accounts at large, which causeth me to omit some passages; but you shall have shortly a larger description, as soon as we proceed further in our affairs, nothing hindering the same but the damned stop which the heretical Synod put unto our late Petition, against the toleration of tender consciences.

* Nominally and by profession a *Baptist*, or as they were then called, an *Anabaptist*.

"We humbly conclude, ever testifying our due and promised obedience to the Fraternity of the Holy Society of Jesus, whose undertakings to the advancement of the Mother-Church, his Holiness, and the propagation of the faith thereof, we ever intreat the Blessed Trinity, the holy blessed Virgin Mary, the Mother of God, Archangels, Angels, Cherubims and Seraphims, Patriarchs, Prophets, St. Peter, St. Paul, the Apostles, Martyrs, Saints, and all the heavenly host to assist and bless, &c. Amen.

"London, April 6, 1645." "J. FAGAN."

Important additional testimony as to the proceedings of the Papists in England at this time is to be found in a letter by Archbishop Bramhall (then Bishop of Derry) in 1654 to Archbishop Usher, giving him an account of the information that had come to him, upon indubitable evidence, as to the large concern which the Papists had in *promoting the civil war and the death of the king*, and the way in which they were then pursuing a similar course for similar ends. This letter was first printed in Parr's Life and Letters of Usher in 1685, and the whole impression of the book was seized by order of James II. on account of its insertion,* and the book subsequently published without it. It is stated in this letter:—

"It plainly appears that in the year 1646, by order from Rome, above 100 of the Romish clergy were sent into England, consisting of English, Scotch, and Irish, who had been educated in France, Italy, Germany, and Spain; part of these within the several schools then appointed for their instruction. In each of these Romish nurseries these scholars were taught several handicraft trades and callings, as their ingenuities were most bending; besides their orders or functions of that Church. They have many yet at Paris a-fitting to be sent over, who twice in the week oppose one the other; one pretending Presbytery, the other Independency; some Anabaptism, and the others contrary tenets, dangerous and prejudicial to the Church of England, and to all the

* See Evelyn's Diary, under date April 18, 1686.

Reformed here abroad. But they [*i.e.* the Reformed] are wisely preparing to prevent their designs; which I heartily wish were considered in England among the wise there." He proceeds to state that each emissary had several names given him, so that upon discovery in one place he might go to another and assume a different name, and all were to be in constant correspondence with those who sent them; and that in England they were to pass themselves off as " poor Christians that formerly fled beyond seas for their religion's sake, and are now returned with glad news [gladness] to enjoy their liberty of conscience." The letter proceeds thus :—" The hundred men that went over in 1646 were most of them soldiers in the Parliament's army, and were daily to correspond with those Romanists in our late King's army that were lately at Oxford, and pretended to fight for his sacred Majesty; for at that time there were some Roman Catholics who did not know the design a-contriving against our Church and State of England. But the year following, 1647, many of those Romish Orders, who came over the year before, were in consultation together, knowing each other; and those of the King's party asking some, Why they took with the Parliament's side, and asking others, Whether they were bewitched to turn Puritans, not knowing the design; but at last secret Bulls and Licences being produced by those of the Parliament's side, it was declared between them, There was no better design to confound the Church of England, than by *pretending liberty of conscience.* It was argued then that England would be a second Holland, a Commonwealth; and if so, what would become of the King? It was answered, Would to God it were come to that point. It was again replied, Yourselves have preached so much against Rome and his Holiness, that Rome and her Romanists will be little the better for that change. But it was answered, You shall have mass sufficient for a hundred thousand in a short space, and the governors never the wiser. Then some of the mercifullest of the Romanists said, This cannot be done unless the King die, upon which argument the Romish

Orders thus licensed, and in the Parliament army, wrote unto their several Convents, but especially to the Sorbonists, whether it may be scrupled to make away our late godly King and his Majesty his Son, our King and Master; who, blessed be God, hath escaped their Romish snares laid for him. It was returned from the Sorbonists, that it was lawful for Roman Catholics to work *changes in Governments for the Mother-Church's advancement*, and chiefly in an heretical kingdom; and so *lawfully make away the king*. Thus much to my knowledge have I seen and heard since my leaving your Lordship, which I thought very requisite to inform your Grace; for myself would hardly have credited these things, had not mine eyes seen sure evidence of the same."*

A confirmation of these accounts will be found in a work of Dr. Peter Du Moulin, first published soon after the Restoration, in which he says:—

"When the businesses of the late bad times are once ripe for a history, and time the bringer of truth hath discovered the mysteries of iniquity, and the depths of Satan, which have wrought so much crime and mischief, it will be found, that the late Rebellion was raised and fostered by the arts of the Court of Rome; that Jesuits professed themselves Independent, as not depending on the Church of England, and fifth-monarchy men, that they might pull down the English monarchy, and that in the Committees for the destruction of the King and the Church they had their spies and their agents. The Roman priest and confessor is known, who when he saw the fatal stroke given to our holy King and Martyr, flourished with his sword, and said, Now the greatest enemy that we have in the world is gone."†

And he gives several proofs of the joy with which the intelligence of the King's death was received by the Romanists,‡

---

* Bramhall's Works, Oxf. 1842, vol. i. p. xcv. et seq. The letter is also to be found in "Foxes and Firebrands," pt. 3, pp. 164—169, and in the Harleian Miscellany, vii. 542, &c.

† A vindication of the sincerity of the Protestant Religion in point of obedience to sovereigns, in answer to Philanax Anglicus, by P. du Moulin, D.D., Canon of Canterbury 4th edn. 1679. 4to, p. 58

‡ Ib. pp. 58, 59; 66, 67.

and states that the friars contended with the Jesuits for "the glory" of having promoted "that great achievement."*

And he declares himself able to prove, "whensoever authority will require it," "that the year before the King's death a select number of English Jesuits were sent from their whole party in England, first to Paris, to consult with the Faculty of Sorbon, then altogether Jesuited; to whom they put this question in writing: That seeing the State of England was in a likely posture to change Government, whether it was lawful for the Catholics to work that change, for the advancing and securing of the Catholic cause in England, *by making away the King*, whom there was no hope to turn from his heresy. Which was answered *affirmatively*. After which the same persons went to Rome; where the same question being propounded and debated, it was concluded by the Pope and his Council, that it was *both lawful and expedient for the Catholics to promote that alteration of State*."† And in answer to the vague denials of the charge by some Romanists he says,—"I have defied them now seventeen years to call me in question before our Judges, and so I do still," and testifies his readiness at any time to justify his statements, when called upon by public authority to do so.‡ And he gives a letter from Sir W. Morrice, Secretary of State to Charles II., written when he first published this charge, in which that high officer of State, after alluding to the necessity of caution in what he said in his position, writes thus,—"But this I may say safely, and will do it confidently, that many arguments did create a violent suspicion, very near convincing evidences, that the irreligion of the Papists was chiefly guilty of the murther of that excellent Prince, the odium whereof they would now file to the account of the Protestant religion."§

"Mr. Prynne's intelligence," he adds, "confirmed mine. He saith (True and Perfect Narrative, p. 46) that our late excellent King having assented, in the Treaty of the Isle of

---

* "A Vindication, &c." p. 67. † Ib. p. 59.
‡ Ib. pp. 61, 62.   § Ib. pp. 64, 65.

Wight, to pass five strict Bills against Popery, *the Jesuits in France, at a general meeting there, presently resolved to bring him to justice and take off his head, by the power of their friends in the army:* as the King himself was certified by an express from thence, and wished to provide against it, but two days before his removal by the army from the Isle of Wight to his execution."*

"In pursuance of this order from Rome for the pulling down both the Monarch and the Monarchy of England, many Jesuits came over who took several shapes, to go about their work, but most of them took party in the army. About thirty of them or their disciples were met by a Protestant gentleman between Roan and Dieppe, to whom they said (taking him for one of their party) that they were going into England, and would take arms in the Independent army, and endeavour to be agitators."†

One more testimony may be added to these:—

"When the late king [Charles I.] was murdered, Master Henry Spotswood, riding casually that way just as his head was cut off, espied the Queen's Confessor there on horseback, in the habit of a trooper, drawing forth his sword and flourishing it over his own head in triumph (as others then did); at which Mr. Spotswood being much amazed, and being familiarly acquainted with the Confessor, rode up to him, and said, 'O father, I little thought to have found you here, or any of your profession, at such a sad spectacle.' To which he answered, 'That there were at least forty or more priests and Jesuits there present on horseback, besides himself.'"‡

Richard Baxter has dwelt at some length on the same subject in his "Key for Catholics," 1659, 4to, in which he devotes the 45th chapter to pointing out the fraud of the Papists "in seeking to divide the Protestants among themselves, or to break them into sects, or poison the ductile sort with heresies, and then to draw them to some odious prac-

---

* "A Vindication, &c.," p. 65. † Ib. pp. 65, 66.
‡ Prynne's Brief Necessary Vindication, p. 45, *as quoted in* Foxes and Firebrands, Pt. iii. pp. 163-164.

tices, to cast a disgrace on the Protestant cause." (p. 313.) In his remarks on this subject he observes, as one living at the time and knowing well the general state of feeling in the kingdom, "I do therefore leave it here to posterity . . . . . that it was utterly against the mind and thoughts of Protestants, and those that they called Puritans, to put the king to death." (p. 323.) And to the question what the Papists get by all this, he justly replies,—"By this means our Councils, armies, Churches, have been divided or much broken. By this trick they have engaged the minds and tongues of many (and their hands if they had power) against the Ministry, which is the enemy that standeth in their way. They have thus weakened us by the loss of our former adherents. . . . . By this they have got agents ready for mischievous designs, as hath been lately too manifest. By this they have cast a reproach upon our profession, as if we had no unity or consistence, but were *vertiginous for want of the Roman pillar to rest upon.* By this they have loosened and disaffected the common people, *to see so many minds and ways, and hear so much contending,* and have loosed them from their former steadfastness, and made them ready for a new impression. Yea, by this means they have the opportunity of predicating their own pretended unity, and hereby have drawn many to their Church of late. All this have they got at this one game."*

And in his "Life" he mentions a fact which confirms the statements of Du Moulin, namely that a Mr. Atkins, brother of Judge Atkins, when abroad, made the acquaintance of a priest who had been Governor of one of the Romish Colleges in Flanders, and meeting this priest in London "a little after the King was beheaded," was privately told by him, "That there were thirty of them here in London, who by instructions from Cardinal Mazarine, did take care of such affairs, and had sate in Council and debated the question,

---

* Pp. 329, 330. See also his 46th chapter on "Another practical fraud of the Papists in hiding themselves and their religion, that they may do their work with the more advantage."

Whether the King should be put to death or not, and that it was carried in the affirmative, and there were but two voices for the negative, which was his own and another's: and that for his part he could not concur with them, as foreseeing what misery this would bring upon this country." "I would not print it," adds Baxter, "without fuller attestation, lest it should be a wrong to the Papists. But when the King was restored and settled in peace, I told it occasionally to a Privy Councillor, who not advising me to meddle any further in it, because the King *knew enough of Mazarine's designs already*, I let it alone. But about this time I met with Dr. Thomas Goad, and occasionally mentioning such a thing, he told me that he was familiarly acquainted with Mr. Atkins, and would know the certainty of him, whether it were true: and not long after, meeting him again, he told me that he spoke with Mr. Atkins, and that he assured him that it was true, but he was loth to meddle in the publication of it."*

It is clear from these documents that much of the blood shed at that unhappy period of civil strife and religious dissension lies at the door of the Church of Rome; and we see from them, that fraud, deceit, and crime of every kind are instruments of which she unhesitatingly avails herself to bring mankind under her yoke; seducing her agents into the belief that they are benefiting "holy Mother Church," and doing God service.

After the death of the king, finding themselves probably as far off as ever from the attainment of the object they had in view, the Papists proceeded secretly in the same course as before. And the following testimony was borne to their proceedings in 1654:—

"1. That there are multitudes of Romish emissaries and vermin now residing and wandering up and down freely amongst us, to seduce and divide the people, by setting up new sects and separate congregations in all places, and

---

* Baxter's Narrative of his Life. Published by Sylvester. Lond. 1696. fol. Pt. 2, pp. 373, 374. The evident leaning of the Court towards Popery quite accounts for the indisposition to "meddle" with these matters.

broaching new notions and opinions of all sorts, or old heresies or blasphemies. . . . . .

" 2. That they are the chief speakers and rulers in most separate congregations. . . . .

" 3. That they have their several Missions and Directions into all parts from their Generals and Superiors of their respective Orders, residing commonly in London, (*where they have a Consistory and Council sitting, that rules all the affairs of the things of England*) besides fixed officers in every Diocese, and are all fore-acquainted both with the places and times of their several Missions. . . . . .

" 4. That the Pope's and these his Emissaries' chief endeavours are to draw the people from our churches, public congregations, ordinances, ministers and religion, and *to divide and tumble us into as many sects and separate conventicles as they have Popish Orders; and thereby into as many Civil Parties and Factions as possibly they can, to ruin us thereby.*

" 5. That by this their new stratagem and liberty, they have (under the disguises of being Quakers, Seekers, Anabaptists, Independents, Ranters, Dippers, Anti-Trinitarians, Anti-Scripturists, and the like) gained more proselytes and disciples, and done more harm in eight or nine years space to *the Church and Realm of England,* more prejudice, dishonour and scandal to our religion and ministers, than ever they did by saying Mass, or preaching, printing, or any point of the grossest Popery in 80 years time heretofore. And if not speedily, diligently restrained, repressed, will soon *utterly overturn both our Church, Religion, Ministry, and State too in conclusion, having already brought them to sad confusions and distractions.*"*

The restoration of the Stuart family in the person of Charles II. inspired the Papists with fresh hopes. The tendency of the King's mind, (even if he had not been reconciled before his arrival in England to the Church of

---

* Foxes and Firebrands, Pt. 2, pp. 144—146.

Rome, which is most probable,*) and the secret promises he had made to his Popish allies, were all well known at Rome; and the emissaries of Rome were diligent and active during his reign in secretly paving the way for the re-establishment of Popery in this country; and but for the decided Anti-Popish feelings of the Nation, the Church of Rome would again have placed England under its yoke. The King well knew what had been the plots of the Romanists against his father, and his plan of action seems to have been, *secretly* to aid and encourage the Popish conspirators against the religion and liberties of the nation, and so secure himself against their hostility, while *outwardly*, for the preservation of his crown, he professed Protestantism, and did what was necessary, even in opposition to the Papists, to satisfy or at least keep quiet his Protestant subjects. Such was the fruit of the Popish teaching to which he had been exposed.

During the whole of this reign, therefore, the chief agent of the Church of Rome, under the disguise of a profession of Protestantism, was the king himself. And the first object aimed at for the purpose of ultimately effecting the re-establishment of Popery was what was called a general toleration. This was to be the first step towards the attainment of the end which we know from their own testimony the Papists had in view.

So far as respects the free exercise of their religion, I offer no remark, still less censure, upon any open, honest, and straightforward efforts to obtain it. But what I wish to point out is, not merely that this was sought for as a mere instrument towards attaining the real object they had in view, but what was *their mode of action for accomplishing their purposes*. This continued to be, as it had all along been, and still is, *the division of Protestants among themselves* by all kinds of subtle artifices, disguised agents, and faithless counsels.

The great effort therefore of the Papists at the commence-

---

* See Hallam's Const. Hist. 4th ed. vol. ii. p. 41, *note*. Bp. Burnet (Hist. of his own Times, i. 273) asserts that King Charles admitted his being a Papist to the Prince of Orange (afterwards William III.) in 1669.

ment of this reign was to make the breach as wide as possible between the Church and the Protestant Nonconformists, and so increase the number of the latter as to enable the Crown, without exciting public discontent, to grant a dispensation from the effects of the penal laws, which should include the Papists within its scope.

"It was the strength of Popery," says Bishop Kennet, "that now [*i.e.* in 1662] chiefly made the separation of Protestants from the Church of England."* The Act of Uniformity, he tells us, would have prospered far better "if the Ministers inclined to separation had not been encouraged in it by the connivance of the Court and the promised indulgence of the king."† And Archbishop Tenison, in his Discourse concerning the Ecclesiastical Commission in 1689, tells us, that "the mystery of Popery did even then [*i.e.* in 1661] work" to prevent reformation and union.

The testimony of Bishop Burnet is still more full and express; he says,—"Though he [the King] put on an outward appearance of moderation, yet he was in another and deeper laid design, to which the heat of these men proved subservient, *for bringing in of Popery.* . . . . It was thought a toleration was the only method for *setting it a-going all the nation over.* And nothing could make a toleration for Popery pass, but the having great bodies of men put out of the Church, and put under severe laws, which should force them to move for a toleration, and should make it reasonable to grant it to them. And it was resolved, that whatever should be granted of that sort should go in so large a manner, that Papists should be comprehended within it. *So the Papists had this generally spread among them, that they should oppose all propositions for comprehension, and should animate the Church party to maintain their ground against all the sectaries.* And in that point they seemed zealous for the Church. But at the same time, they spoke of toleration, as necessary both for the peace and quiet of the nation and for the encouragement

---

* History, 2nd ed., vol. iii. p. 267. † History, vol. iii. p. 262.

of trade. And with this the Duke [of York] was so possessed, that he declared himself a most violent enemy to comprehension and as zealous for toleration."*

And speaking of a conversation he had with a secular Romish priest, Peter Walsh, who he says was the "honestest and learnedest man I ever knew among them," and "knew well the methods of the Jesuits and other missionaries," he adds,—"He told me often, *there was nothing which the whole Popish party feared more than an union of those of the Church of England with the Presbyterians;* they knew, we grew the weaker, the more our breaches were widened; and that the more we were set against one another, we would mind them the less. *The Papists had two maxims, from which they never departed: the one was* TO DIVIDE US: *and the other was, to keep themselves united,* and either to set on an indiscriminated toleration, or a general prosecution; for so we loved to soften the harsh word of *persecution*. And he observed, not without great indignation at us for our folly, that we, instead of uniting among ourselves, and dividing them, according to their maxims, did all we could to keep them united, and to disjoint our own body."†

Thus the influence of the Papists was exerted to increase as much as they could the ranks of the Nonconformists, and make them as formidable a body in opposition to the Church as possible; and then to induce the King to grant them toleration by assuming a power of dispensing with the penal laws, which it was hoped the Nonconformists would be thankful to acquiesce in, and which would include a toleration for the Popish party. But in this they were disappointed, the Protestant spirit of the Parliament being too strong to allow the King to carry out this design.

In the course of a few years, however, when the Parliament became more inclined than they had previously been to measures of *comprehension*, the Court party with the Papists, foreseeing that if the Church and the Nonconformists

---

* Hist. of his Own Times, vol. i. p. 179. † Ibid. p. 195.

came to a good understanding between themselves, both would be united against them, and no chance would remain of a toleration of Popery, changed their tactics and urged the execution of the laws against Nonconformists. "The Court," says Hallam, "entertained great hopes from the depressed condition of the Dissenters, whom it was intended to bribe with that toleration under a Catholic regimen, which they could so little expect from the Church of England. Hence the Duke of York was always *strenuous against schemes of comprehension, which would invigorate the Protestant interest and promote conciliation. With the opposite view of rendering a union among Protestants impracticable, the rigorous Episcopalians were encouraged underhand to prosecute the Nonconformists.*"*

"As it had been formerly," says Kennet, "the interest of the Papists to promote indulgence and toleration to the Protestant dissenters, that under the effects of such a liberty they might shelter themselves and weaken the Church of England, so now, upon a turn of affairs, they changed their opinion, or at least their measures, for that party now encouraged the severe prosecution of the Protestant dissenters, thereby to take off the edge of the laws from themselves, and to divert the zeal of the members of the Church of England against their brethren in separation from them, and so to irritate and alienate the hearts of all Protestants from one another."†

And the better to carry on their designs, they managed, as before, to get themselves appointed, *under the profession of Protestantism*, to offices and employments of all kinds, and even to ecclesiastical preferments.

"Under the Duke's protection," says Kennet, "many of the Roman Catholics were publicly encouraged and preferred; and some others of them acted a more secret part in assuming the name of Protestants, and *under that disguise thrusting themselves into places and employments.* Among

---

* Hallam, vol. ii. p. 82. † Kennet, vol. iii. p. 381.

these *one at least crept into a cure of souls*, one John Duffey, a Scotchman, who obtained the Rectory of Raile in Essex; and who, upon information of his character given to the Council Board, was sent for into custody; but on the 5th of December [1682] he made his escape from one of his Majesty's messengers."*

But perhaps the most remarkable proof that occurs during this reign of the extent of the duplicity and fraudulence to which those who are under the influence of Popish principles may be carried, is in the secret Treaty concluded with France in 1670. While the king was professing Protestantism and a desire to uphold the Protestant faith and discourage Romanism, he and the duke of York held a consultation with three leading Papists (Clifford, Arlington, and Lord Arundel of Wardour) on the 25th of January, 1669, "*to discuss the ways and methods fit to be taken for the advancement of the Catholic religion in these kingdoms.* The King spoke earnestly, and with tears in his eyes. After a long deliberation, it was agreed that there was no better way to accomplish this purpose than through France, the house of Austria being in no condition to give any assistance." And accordingly a secret treaty, having this object in view, was negotiated with France, and signed in the course of the following year at Dover; and the secret was so well kept, that though the strongest suspicions were entertained in Parliament and throughout the nation that some plots of the kind were in agitation, and that the Court was not to be trusted, the real text of the treaty was never *published* till the latter end of the last century. In the treaty there is of course no direct engagement that the Roman Catholic religion shall be that of the National Church in England, but that this was the object of it is undeniable, and the proofs are stated by Hallam.† And if anything were wanting in the evidence of this afforded by the correspondence and negotiations that took place at the period, it would be supplied by Coleman's letters, seized some years after.‡

---

* Kennet, vol. iii. p. 398.   † Constit. Hist. vol. ii. pp. 76—81.
‡ See State Trials, vol. vii. p. 1. Kennet, ed. 1719, vol. iii. pp. 327, 328; 337; 351, 352. Burnet, vol. i. p. 427. Hallam, vol. ii. p. 116.

It was believed by the Court (Mr. Hallam says) and probably with reason, that many who were nominally Protestants were secretly inclined to Romanism, and would gladly embrace it if circumstances favoured its profession; and that even some of the clergy would without much hesitation take the same course. "It was the constant policy of the Romish priests *to extenuate the differences between the two Churches, and to throw the main odium of the schism on the Calvinistic sects.* And many of the Anglicans, in abhorrence of Protestant Nonconformists, played into the hands of the common enemy."* Such is Mr. Hallam's remark, written previous to the recent rise of the Romanizing party in our Church.

It is remarkable how identical have been the tactics of the Romish party throughout all their various efforts for the re-establishment of Popery in this country.

On the question of the credibility of the evidence for the alleged plot of 1678, I shall not here enter.† The existence of *a* secret Popish plot against the religion and liberties of the country, in which the highest personages in the realm were engaged, is (as already shown) a matter of history; and this is amply sufficient for our present purpose.

Speaking of the supposed plot of 1678, Mr. Hallam justly remarks,—"It is first to be remembered, that there was really and truly a Popish plot in being, though not that which Titus Oates and his associates pretended to reveal—not merely in the sense of Hume, who, arguing from the general spirit of proselytism in that religion, says there is a perpetual conspiracy against all governments, Protestant, Mahometan, and Pagan, but—*one alert, enterprising, effective, in direct operation against the established Protestant religion in England.* In this plot the King, the Duke of York, and the King of France were chief conspirators; the Romish priests, and

* Ibid. pp. 81, 82.
† The plot was one that threatened the life of the King, who, though he secretly favoured the Romanists, was too careful of his crown and his pleasures to do anything likely to put them in peril. The Romanists therefore, knowing that they could rely upon the open and direct aid of his successor, were very probably desirous enough of getting rid of him, and hastening the accession of James II.

especially the Jesuits, were eager co-operators. Their machinations and their hopes, long suspected and in a general sense known, were divulged by the seizure and publication of Coleman's letters. 'We have here,' he says in one of these, 'a mighty work upon our hands, no less than the conversion of three kingdoms, and by that perhaps the utter subduing of a pestilent heresy, which has a long time domineered over this Northern world. There were never such hopes since the death of our queen Mary as now in our days. God has given us a prince, who is become (I may say by miracle) zealous of being the author and instrument of so glorious a work; but the opposition we are sure to meet with is also like to be great; so that it imports us to get all the aid and assistance we can.' These letters were addressed to Father la Chaise, confessor of Louis XIV., and displayed an intimate connection with France for the great purpose of *restoring Popery.*"*

It pleased God, however, that the hopes of the Papists should be again disappointed. *The great body of the nation and of its representatives in Parliament were sincere and earnest Protestants,* and though there might be among the clergy those who used language which indicated a greater sympathy with some of the doctrines of the Church of Rome than was strictly consistent with the Formularies of our Church, the general feeling among them seems to have been of a contrary kind; and when the controversy fairly commenced on the accession of James II., it was sustained by the leading clergy of our Church with a zeal, ability, and perseverance which have made the anti-Popish publications of that day a complete armoury for subsequent combatants in the same field. The efforts of the Romanists, though secretly aided by the King himself and the Duke his brother, were successfully counteracted and nullified by the strong Protestant feeling of the country; and Charles II. died leaving to his brother the task of carrying out their design of re-establishing Popery among us as the national faith.

* Ibid. vol. ii. pp. 115, 116.

The efforts of James II. to accomplish this object, I need not here describe. Whatever their character may be considered to be, as far as the legality of them is concerned, they are certainly a shade better than those we have been contemplating, as they were far more free from the guilt of dissimulation and hypocrisy. He professed himself a Papist, and openly gave all the protection and encouragement he could to the Popish party, who under such circumstances needed no disguise to enable them to carry on their designs.

Again the Protestant feelings of the Nation enabled it to triumph over the assaults of the Popish faction, and the Revolution placed upon the throne a sincere Protestant, and established the Protestant faith and Protestant principles upon a secure and lasting basis.

The agents of Rome were no doubt at work to a certain extent in this country, throughout the whole of the last century, especially the former part of it; but, comparatively speaking, their efforts were of a partial and languid kind. The theological storms which were so rife throughout the whole of the preceding century seem to have been succeeded by a lull, in which the vessel of the Faith was becalmed, and remained almost motionless. Popery and Protestantism were both to a great extent sleeping at their posts. The dawn of the present century, whatever may have been the cause, roused both into renewed life and action. As far as Popery is concerned, the impulse was probably given to it in this country by the discussions caused by the Act of Union with Ireland, which was said to have been rendered palatable to its opponents by promises of what was called Roman Catholic Emancipation, and which certainly led to earnest efforts to effect such emancipation. The hopes of the Romanists were thus again roused; and from the commencement of this century, they have laboured steadily and with gradually increasing strength and success to propagate their views, and obtain for themselves an advantageous political position in the country. For some years I believe this was done by open and avowed Papists, and, so far, fairly and honestly whatever we may think of the controversial artifices by which the real tenets of the Church of Rome were disguised and "explained" to give them a plausible appearance to a Protestant nation. But from the period of the passing of the Roman Catholic Emancipation Act, if not before, the old mode of action of the Jesuits has been renewed in this country, and we have been exposed to the arts and intrigues of a body of men scattered over the face of the land, under various disguises, thoroughly unscrupulous, and capable of every fraud, deceit, and iniquity by which they may imagine that the cause of "Mother-Church" is likely to be promoted.

How just the warning given by Southey, when the question of Roman Catholic Emancipation (as it was called) was under discussion:—"It would be a solecism in policy were we to entrust those persons with power in the State, who are bound in conscience to use it for subverting the Church, for undoing the work of the Reformation and of the Revolution, for bringing us again into spiritual bondage, and re-establishing that system of superstition, idolatry, and persecution, from which the sufferings of our martyrs, and the wisdom of our ancestors, by God's blessing, delivered us. Far as we may think them from it, this is the consummation upon which their designs, as well as their desires, are bent."*

To look upon Popery as if it was a harmless form of Christianity, *deserving equal privileges with every other form*, is a fatal delusion, which must be destructive to the peace and welfare of every Protestant nation that acts upon it.

The first reflection which naturally forces itself upon the mind, in reviewing the practices of Popery in this country since the Reformation, is, What a proof is here afforded us of the *corrupt character* of the Papal system of Christianity. The practices of which we have been giving an account, were not those of unauthorized individuals, inflamed

---

* Southey's Vindiciæ Eccles. Anglic., *Preface.*

by an indiscreet zeal, for which they alone were responsible, to promote the interests of their Church, but efforts patronized by the highest Authorities of that Church, the result of counsels deliberately planned and directed by the Pope and his chief cardinals. Earnest vehemence in defence of what is believed to be the truth is intelligible. Even violence in its behalf, utterly opposed as it is to the precepts and example of our Blessed Lord, may be reconcileable, in consideration of the infirmity of human nature, with sincere belief and a desire to promote the cause and kingdom of Christ. But the iniquitous deceit by which doctrines known to be false and dangerous are widely disseminated, and the divisions of Christendom multiplied and exasperated; the deliberate dissimulation and falsehood practised by men assuming a lying exterior for the purpose of deception; the faithless and fraudulent counsels instilled into the ears of confiding and unsuspecting parties, suited to their respective stations, offices, and capacities, to lead them to acts productive of consequences which they would deprecate—all done for the sake of damaging a rival Church, and throwing a kingdom that will not own the authority of the Pope into a state of confusion, are practices which I will boldly affirm are irreconcileable with the existence of any degree of fellowship with Christ, or membership among those whom He will own at a future day.

And it must be remembered, that, according to her own testimony, the Church of Rome is in all her tenets and principles *unchangeable*. What she was in the 17th century, that she is now, and that she will be, if permitted to continue, in the 20th century. Any apparent change is due only to her being fettered by circumstances, and will last only where and as long as those circumstances remain. The delusion of there having been any change in her exclusive, intolerant, and persecuting principles is opposed to her own testimony respecting herself.

The destruction of the Reformed Church of England has been, as the evidence above given shows, the great object of her ambition ever since it first started into existence. Could she but bring that Church again into subjection to the Pope, and make it the supporter and propagator of Romanism, the chief bulwark of the Reformation would be destroyed, and the cause of the Papacy obtain a vantage ground which would give it reasonable hope of a triumph throughout the world.

It is a matter of no little importance to the welfare of our country both in Church and State, that public attention should be directed to this subject. For he must be blind to the signs of the times who can doubt, that the same practices are now, and have been for some years, carried on among us, as were prevalent in this country in the 17th century. It is a fact which no one who knows anything of the state of things in this country can question, that we are "swarming with Jesuits." And all history tells us, what are the great objects they have in view, what the means used to accomplish them, and what the inevitable effects, if not counteracted, in a Protestant State.

It is impossible, I think, to contemplate the present condition of our Church without seeing the remarkable resemblance which it bears to that which existed here about two centuries ago, though, alas! much more ominous of evil, and also how its characteristics point to the identity of the causes from which it springs.

If we look at the secret directions issued to the emissaries of Rome in former times,—as for instance to preach doctrines of all kinds, and then "by degrees to *add to the doctrine by ceremonies*," and "by mixtures of doctrines and by *adding of ceremonies more than be at present permitted*" to bring the "heretical Episcopal Society" of England "*as near the Mother-Church as possible*," to be "more zealous against the Pope" than others, while secretly supporting his cause,* to produce *internal discord* in the Church, so that there may be "the less power to oppose the Church of

---

* See pp. 8, 9, above.

Rome,"* and all the other similar counsels we find in the documents given above,—and then compare them with what has been taking place in our Church during the last few years, we can have, I think, little doubt, judging even from this consideration alone, of the causes that have been at work among us to produce the results we now see.

The first part of Rome's work has been already accomplished, in the production of a degree of strife, discord, and confusion, both in Church and State, which threatens consequences of serious import to the peace and prosperity of the country. And already we hear the voice of Rome taking advantage of the state of things it has itself caused, and alluring us to herself by proclaiming the blessings of the peace and unity we should enjoy under her shadow, in the following syren strains :—

"It seems to me that the happiest and the most blessed condition of a people is to be *perfectly united in religion*. If there could be one faith, one heart, one mind, one worship, one altar, round which the whole population is gathered, *as I see it in Ireland*, with very little to disturb it, such would be the happiest condition of a people. Religious unity, or unity of faith, is the greatest gift of God to men; and that because, first of all, it is *a pledge of truth, universally known and believed*, and that one truth which *admits no division and no contradiction;* next, because it is a guarantee of universal peace—*no controversy and no conflict, and no divisions of households, no intestine and domestic strife;* and lastly, because it insures the inheritance of truth and of faith to posterity to be hereafter born. Whereas, where the religious unity of a people is divided and fractured, truth escapes, and children are born, generation after generation, disinherited of the heirloom of Christianity. For these reasons, I do desire from my heart to see the unity of faith spreading more and more among us. This I believe to be the best state of a people. I believe the *worst state of a people to be one of conflict, controversy, religious strife, theo-*

* See p. 12 above.

logical bitterness. It seems to me that the plagues of Egypt are the types of such a state."*

Beautiful picture of the harmony and peace which Popery brings with it, where it is allowed to reign triumphant! And the speaker tells us, that we have only got to go to Ireland to see it. We are obliged to him for pointing us to an *example*, because we may hence judge somewhat of the true nature of the Paradisiacal state to which Popery would introduce us. And I doubt whether Englishmen will much care for further information as to the happy condition in which they would thus be placed, when told that it is like that enjoyed by the Roman Catholics of Ireland,—so much love and knowledge of the truth, so much true spiritual worship, so marked a manifestation of the spirit of Christianity in all the practical duties of life, such delightful peace and harmony, such well-grounded tranquillity of mind in the prospect of death and eternity. Who would not be a Papist, and wish his country to be under the rule of the Pope as Christ's Vicar, to obtain such blessings!

I fear, however, that there are many among us, in high position and of great influence, who are quite unconscious, and in truth hide from themselves the fact, of the dangers to which we are exposed from the machinations of the Church of Rome. Acting themselves according to the principles they profess, and not realizing the presence of men whose real objects are at variance with their professions, they argue upon the events that are taking place around them, and draw conclusions as to their probable results, in a way which, if all others were acting in a similar manner, and there were no unscrupulous agents and marked emissaries of superstition working deceitfully for the overthrow of a pure faith, would have much weight. Their whole train of reasoning is founded upon notions that completely ignore the fact of there being scattered among us a set of men,

---

* Dr. Manning's Address at the Thirteenth Annual *Réunion* of the Roman Catholics of Birmingham, on January 15th, 1867, as reported in the *Times* of Jan. 17.

exteriorly of the most religious kind (like the Pharisees of old), and perhaps themselves imbued with the notion that they are doing God service, whose end and object is to uproot the pure faith and worship of Christ, as re-established among us at the Reformation, and who believe it to be consistent with Christian duty, and even meritorious, to use any means likely to accomplish this end; and that among those means is the employment of disguised Romish agents, making their way into offices and employments of various kinds, even in our Church, and using weak and ill-informed and indifferent and disaffected Protestants, clergy and laity, as tools for the accomplishment of their designs. When a body of men of this kind are insidiously working under the surface throughout a kingdom, no judgment can be formed as to what course events may take. All ordinary calculations are baffled by the difference between apparent tendencies and real designs. And *the character and interests* both of *individuals* and *the community at large* are almost at the mercy of Rome.

I have often thought, when reading the remarks of some simple-hearted and ingenuous Protestant upon the present state of things among us, how the wily followers of that corrupt Church, which has been for three centuries struggling to regain its lost ascendancy in this country, would laugh at the simplicity of their Protestant opponents; and when they saw how completely the lessons of history and the discovered arts of former times were ignored and forgotten, would redouble the crafty machinations by which they sought to accomplish their objects.

The truth is, a Protestant Church is no match for a body of men of this kind. The principle of action in the former is one which leaves it exposed in various ways to the insidious assaults of the latter. In the former, every man who is *true to his principles* avoids everything like deceit and underhand dealing, even if they might seem likely to advance what he believes to be the cause of truth. Among the latter, in a Protestant country, these are the chief weapons of their warfare, and weapons against which their Protestant opponents have no defence. They disdain to use them, and almost disbelieve the use of them by others. The influence which the agents of Rome had here in the middle of the 17th century, in propagating erroneous doctrines, instigating to strife and bloodshed, and misleading in various ways the minds of the people, was, we *now* know, enormous. But, *at the time, scarcely anything was known* of the secret influences that were at work, producing the discord, confusion, and disorder that reigned at that unhappy period.

So it will ever be when a body of men like the Romanists, and especially the Jesuits, are at work in a country to whose faith they are opposed.

Another cause why Protestants are always at a disadvantage when opposed by Romanists, and especially Jesuits, is, that their comparative independence of one another, and their not being united under one directing head, prevent their combination even for the defence of their own principles. No course of united action, requiring and obtaining universal co-operation, and having the maintenance and advance of Protestant principles in view, is ever adopted. This, it must be admitted, is especially the case with a Church in connection with the State. Its official leaders are not real leaders, and practically prevent others from acting as such. And when Popery has obtained such a position in the State as to give it influence in, or with, the Government, effects are discernible, indirect it may be, and perhaps more negative than positive, but of a very real kind, in the Church, far from favourable to its Protestant action. And hence unity of action, even in its own defence, and in the presence of its enemies, is almost hopeless.

Must it not be added, that from our want of acquaintance, as a nation, with all the superstitious mummeries, ignorance, and vice which Popery brings in its train, and the neglect of religious instruction in the education of the young, there is a degree of indifference on the subject which strongly contrasts with the earnestness of former times, when the traditions of the corruptions of Popery and its degrading rites and superstitions were fresh in the minds of the nation?

To the present generation among us Popery is presented only in its most attractive garb. Its form of worship, pleasing to some from its very novelty, is elaborately adapted to the gratification of the senses. Its doctrines are toned down and "explained" in the style of Gother and Bossuet and Francis a Sancta Clara, to entrap the unwary or ill-instructed Protestant into a belief of their being substantially identical with those of the Church of England. Its language is that of the most ardent piety and devotedness to the cause of God and His Church. When acting in defiance of the first principles of Christian morality, inculcating and practising deceit and falsehood, injustice and violence, its adherents adopt a phraseology which tacitly claims for them the highest place among God's earthly saints. Look to their words only, and the forms and ceremonies with which they burthen themselves, and you would suppose you had got *holy men of God* to deal with, whose precepts and example must be the very best standard you could adopt. What wonder is it that many are misled?

It must be added, that the success which the agents of Rome have met with in our Church, has been such as to increase largely the danger arising from the operations of her direct and commissioned emissaries. These operations have for some years been aided and supplemented (as in former times) by those among us who, though not direct agents of Rome, are almost equally faithless in heart to the doctrines of our Church, and labouring as zealously for its destruction as a Protestant Church, and the abrogation of its Reformed Formularies. I am afraid there is more than one "*Montague*" among us.* We are plainly told by high Romish authority,† that our own clergy are saving the priests of Rome the

---

* See pp. 29—33, above. The name should be spelt, *Mountagu*.
† Dr. Manning, calling himself Archbishop of Westminster.

trouble of endeavouring to spread their doctrines among us by doing so themselves.

The *verbal repudiation* of Romish doctrine by those who are zealously teaching it in our Protestant Church is quite what the documents given above would lead us to expect, not merely from Rome's own disguised agents, but from many others; in some cases from want of knowledge and discrimination between Romish and Protestant doctrine, and in others from motives less creditable. We know from the records of former times, that there may be those, high in *position* and *character*, who may think themselves justified in avowing, *secretly,—" As for the aversion we discover* [*to Romanism*] *in our sermons and printed books, they are things of form, chiefly to humour the populace, and not to be much regarded.*"*

Nor have we any reason, I think, to suppose, that the present generation are less likely to produce those who will take such a method of advancing their doctrines than that which existed here two centuries ago. The most eminent perhaps of the first leaders of the Tractarian party,—on whose memory, though he has now for some years been a member of the Church of Rome, they seem still to dwell almost with rapture, especially for his services for teaching them in Tract XC. to give a Romish interpretation to our Protestant Articles,—started on his career for unprotestantizing the Church of England with the following deliberate statement of his views on the subject of truthfulness. Advocating the " economy" that " sets the truth out to advantage," he tells us, that the Alexandrian father [Clement] *"accurately describes the rules which should guide the Christian in speaking and acting economically." " Towards those who are fit recipients,* both in speaking and living he *harmonizes his profession with his opinions.* He both thinks and speaks the truth, EXCEPT *when consideration is necessary, and then, as a physician for the good of his patients,* HE WILL BE FALSE, OR UTTER A FALSEHOOD, as the sophists say. . . . . Nothing however but *his neighbour's good* will lead him to do this. He *gives himself up for the Church,"* &c.†

---

* See p. 33, above.   † Newman's Arians of the 4th Century, p. 72.

And some years after, when obliged to account, in some way, for the language he had used respecting the Church of Rome, he admits,—"If you ask me how an individual could venture, not simply to hold, but to publish, such views of a Communion so ancient, so widespreading, so fruitful in saints, I answer, that *I said to myself,* '*I am not speaking my own words,* I am but following almost a *consensus* of the divines of my Church. . . . . SUCH VIEWS TOO ARE NECESSARY FOR OUR POSITION.' Yet I have reason to fear still, that such language is to be ascribed, in no small measure, to an impetuous temper, *a hope of approving myself to persons' respect,* and A WISH TO REPEL THE CHARGE OF ROMANISM."*

Can we be surprised, that the author of these statements should also be the author of Tract XC. ?

Is it unfair to estimate others by the standard of their cherished leader, and take these avowals as a measure by which to judge of the value of their professions ?

Dr. Pusey certainly has himself so identified his views with those of Mr. Newman before his reception into the Church of Rome, especially as it respects Tract XC., which he has recently republished, that he at least must be considered as occupying the same position as Mr. Newman did before he left us. The light indeed in which Dr. Pusey has from the commencement of the Tractarian movement regarded those Formularies of our Church to which he has given, and is still obliged to profess, his "*ex animo* consent," may be judged from his Letter to the Archbishop of Canterbury, and other publications issued by him more than twenty years ago ; in which he complains of our "impaired Formularies,"† and admits his "longing to *re-appropriate*" from "the Roman Communion" what our Reformers rejected.‡

Sixteen years ago, *members of his own party*, and zealous friends, addressed him in the following terms :—

"Both by precept and example you have been amongst the most earnest to maintain Catholic principles. By your

---

* Letter, dated Dec. 12, 1842.
† Letter, p. 24 ; or, 3rd ed. p. 20.   ‡ Ibid., p. 15 ; or, 3rd ed. p. 13.

constant and common practice of administering the sacrament of penance; by encouraging everywhere, if not enjoining, auricular confession, and giving special priestly absolution; by teaching the propitiatory sacrifice of the Holy Eucharist, as applicatory of the one sacrifice on the cross, and by adoration of Christ really present on the altar under the form of bread and wine; by your introduction of Roman Catholic books 'adapted to the use of our Church;' by encouraging the use of rosaries and crucifixes, and special devotions to our Lord, as *e.g.* to His Five Wounds; by adopting language most powerfully expressive of our incorporation into Christ, as *e.g.* 'our being inebriated by the blood of our Lord;' by advocating counsels of perfection, and seeking to restore, with more or less fulness, the conventual or monastic life; I say, by the teaching and practice of which this enumeration is *a sufficient type and indication*, you have done much to revive amongst us the system which may be pre-eminently called '*sacramental.*'" And the writer, honestly urging open avowals consistent with this conduct, goes on to plead,—" *Let us no longer have any concealments.* We are now past the time for *reserve* and *economy* in such matters."* But the impatient disciple, having but half embraced the *economical* principles of Tractarianism, and longing to make an honest profession of his true creed, was travelling too quickly for his master, who was in no haste to spoil the game, which he saw was succeeding so admirably, by acting so that his post of advantage within the camp for betraying it ultimately to the enemy might be taken from him. The master therefore remained, to carry on his purposes as before, within the camp, and the impatient disciple, urged by the stings of conscience, passed over to Rome.

Another, who had previously taken the same step, addresses him in language of a similar kind, and thus gives his testimony on the practices adopted with respect to confession and absolution, which may *throw some additional*

---

* Dodsworth's Letter to Dr. Pusey, as quoted in Maskell's Letter, 1850, p. 7.

light on a matter which has recently been the subject of correspondence in the *Times* newspaper :—

" In p. 6 of your letter to Mr. Richards you blame Mr. Dodsworth for having said, in his published letter to you, that you have ' enjoined' auricular confession ; and you say that you could not *enjoin* auricular confession. Suffer me to say, that in connexion with the other words of the same sentence, Mr. Dodsworth's use of the word *enjoin* was just and reasonable. He does not use it simply and without limitation ; he says that you have ' encouraged, if not enjoined' auricular confession : by which it is evident that, in the sense of compulsion, he knew, as well as yourself, you *could not* possibly enjoin auricular confession. *And he knew also,* AS I KNOW, *that to say merely that you have encouraged it, would fall as far short of what your actual practice is, as the word* ENJOIN, *in the sense of* COMPELLING, *would exceed it. He knew that you have done more than encourage confession in very many cases : that you have warned people of the danger of deferring it, have insisted on it as the only remedy, have pointed out the inevitable dangers of the neglect of it, and have promised the highest blessings in the observance, until you had* BROUGHT PENITENTS IN FEAR AND TREMBLING UPON THEIR KNEES BEFORE YOU.

" There are some other parts of your letter to Mr. Richards, which, I must own, have somewhat more than startled me. I have begun almost to doubt the accuracy of my memory, or that I could *ever have understood the commonest rules of plain-speaking upon very solemn mysteries and duties of the Christian faith.* I mean such passages as these : ' We are not to obtrude, nor to offer our services ; not to set up ourselves as guides, or depreciate others ; we are to be passive, ready to minister to any who ' come' to us, but not to cause confusion and heartburning by intruding, through any act or word of ours, into the ministry of others.' . . . . ' In like way, when *residing* elsewhere,'—from which of course no one would suppose that *you go from home into other dioceses for the express purpose of receiving auricular confessions*—' when any came to me, I ministered to them. But not having **a**

parochial cure I have not led others to confession.' . . . . .*
Now pray do not misunderstand me; far be it from me to say that I suppose that, in your own heart, you do not believe every word of these sentences to be strictly and verbally true: WHAT I DO SAY IS, THAT, SO FAR AS I HAVE KNOWN IT, THEY DO NOT IN ANY ADEQUATE OR REAL WAY REPRESENT YOUR PRACTICE. . . . . The Bishop of Exeter would repudiate (I think) with horror the system of particular and detailed inquiry into every circumstance of sin, which, IN CORRECT IMITATION OF THE ROMAN CATHOLIC RULES, YOU DO NOT FAIL TO PRESS. . . . . What, then, let me ask, do you conceive that the Bishop of Exeter would say of PERSONS SECRETLY RECEIVED AGAINST THE KNOWN WILL OF THEIR PARENTS, OF CONFESSIONS HEARD IN THE HOUSES OF COMMON FRIENDS, OR OF CLANDESTINE CORRESPONDENCE TO ARRANGE MEETINGS, UNDER INITIALS, OR IN ENVELOPES ADDRESSED TO OTHER PERSONS? and, more than this, when such confessions are recommended and urged as a part of the spiritual life, and among religious duties; not in order to quiet the conscience before receiving the communion.† Think not that I write all this to give you unnecessary pain: think not that I write it without a feeling of deep pain and sorrow in my own heart. But there is something which tells me, that, on behalf of thousands, this matter should now be *brought before the world plainly, honestly, and fully. I know how heavily the* ENFORCED MYSTERY AND SECRET CORRESPONDENCE REGARDING CONFESSIONS, *in your Communion, has weighed down the minds of many to whom you and others have 'ministered': I know how bitterly it has eaten even as a canker into their very souls: I know how utterly* THE SPECIOUS ARGUMENTS WHICH YOU HAVE URGED, HAVE FAILED TO REMOVE THEIR BURNING SENSE OF SHAME AND OF DECEITFULNESS."‡

Such is the testimony wrung by the voice of conscience from a devoted friend.

* I have omitted much for the sake of brevity.
† The writer adds here the following note:—" A case came within my own knowledge nearly two years ago, in which a young person who hesitated to go to Communion, without previous confession, was directed by Dr. Pusey to go to Communion, and he would receive her confession the following week. This person was in the habit of confessing."
‡ Maskell's Letter to Pusey, 1850, pp. 17—21.

Dr. Pusey has himself given us a very remarkable specimen of the practical operation of the principles of Tractarianism, affecting both himself and Mr. Keble, when giving a reason for Mr. Keble not having himself made the alteration in the "Christian Year" which has been made since his death, and, as is alleged, by his direction, changing the words "present in the heart, *not* in the hands," into "present in the heart, *as* in the hands." Dr Pusey says—"The words *in their strict literal meaning contradict* what had been his belief so long as I have heard him speak on the subject. *So taken* they *affirm* that our Lord gives himself to *the soul of the receiver only*, and is *not present objectively*. This was not John Keble's belief. He himself (as is explained in the *posthumous editions*) understood his own words in the same way as when Holy Scripture says, 'I will have mercy and not sacrifice' (*i.e.*, not sacrifice without mercy), that the objective presence was of no avail unless our Lord was received within, in the cleansed abode of 'the heart.'" "THIS," adds Dr. Pusey, "IS PLAINLY NOT THE OBVIOUS MEANING OF THE WORDS, BUT IT SATISFIED HIM."—(*Times*, Dec. 13, 1866.)

It would be easy to add a hundred-fold to these proofs of the true nature and character of Tractarian principles and practices. But such evidence has been so often placed before the public, that I shall not here repeat it.

It is gratifying to know, that there have been some of the party who, after having been for a time misled, have been enabled to break through the net which an ingenious sophistry had woven around them.

A remarkable pamphlet* was published some years ago by one of these—a pamphlet which clearly manifests how ingenuous and truthful minds writhe under the consciousness of the real character of the system they have been taught—from which I will here give a few extracts.

The author, who tells us that the thoughts he expresses have "pressed on his mind for months, it might be almost

---

* The Morality of Tractarianism: a Letter from one of the people to one of the Clergy. London: W. Pickering. 1850.

said for years past," and that they were "not new to many" of his party, thus describes his experience of Tractarianism:—
"If it should turn out, that this system, instead of having so universally elevating an effect, tends to make those who adopt it *uncandid and prevaricating;* if it gives them *sophistry for faith;* if it *destroys the principle of honour,* and is contrary to that childlike guileless simplicity, that innocence and openness of mind, which surely must be felt to be the one most lovely and distinctive mark of God's children in Christ; then the assertion that Tractarianism is true because its fruit is holiness, does not seem quite unanswerable. Whatever force exists in arguing from its *good* moral results, neither more nor less must be granted, if we discover its moral effect to be *bad. This is what disturbs thousands* whom logic and controversy would never disturb. *It is a feeling which has lurked unexpressed in the hearts of its warmest followers.* NOT ONE OF US BUT MUST OWN IT: NOT ONE BUT HAS WRITHED UNDER THE TORTURE OF DOUBTING, WHETHER, ON THE THRESHOLD OF THIS SYSTEM, WHICH HE EMBRACES TO MAKE HIM HOLY, THERE RESTS NOT THE STAIN AND SEMBLANCE OF A LIE. Is this too harsh a term? But what is the fact? Do we not as Catholics claim to believe doctrines which yet we dare not avow in their plain unmistakeable words? We dare not; for, alas! the Church of England does not give us plain and unmistakeable words in which to avow them: and *if we convince ourselves that she does not rather intend us to avow* THEIR VERY REVERSE, *it is only by a course of explanation which twists her apparently most Protestant statements into a positive sanction of Catholic truth."* (pp. 8, 9.) "The question of subscription does not belong to those who have nothing to subscribe; doubtless the knowledge that our teachers, who deliver to us the various Catholic doctrines which we have regained, have all previously given their *ex animo* consent to articles whose obvious intention, to unlearned minds, was to *oppose* such doctrines, does accustom us to the principle of *ingenious interpretation,* and to a similar mode of thinking and acting, which are the evils I

complain of." " If then we first acknowledge that the only way of holding such truths in the English Church is by the use of *non-natural interpretation*, and then also acknowledge that these truths are the heritage of the people, not the exclusive privilege of the educated classes, we must begin by spreading *the spirit of casuistry* among our village schools and labourers' cottages; we must make our wives and daughters students in scholastic niceties; and in a degree we have done so. *Where we have not, we have left them Protestant; where we have, we have made them* FALSE." (pp. 10, 11.) " We tread the aisle with faltering steps, trying to do as we were bid, and to drown our doubts with *clever prevarications*. We see the priest standing before the altar. ..... It is as if he said, ' I am here offering up the unbloody sacrifice of the very Body and Blood of Christ for the remission of quick and dead. This is what as Catholics we claim to believe. But it is a secret between you and me: I could not teach the people so; it would give offence, seeming contrary to the Prayer Book, though in reality it is not, *because the Article which denies it is not aimed at the doctrine itself, but at the particular way in which once it was taken by the vulgar.* The difference between our doctrine and that received by the Roman branch of the Church Catholic is *entirely verbal: a distinction of terms was all that the Reformers died for, no real distinction of belief.* .... You may adore, for you see everybody kneels; *and though the Church of England says it is idolatry to do so, she meant exactly the reverse;* or, if she did not actually command it, she at any rate permits her children to do what her language calls idolatrous.'" (pp. 16, 17.) "Wonderful sophistry! most solid ground of faith! excellent school for guilelessness and sincerity! admirable preparation for making men holy, and good, and saintly, and everything that is Christian! *except, perhaps, making them* TRUE! Can we any longer believe with the fulness of faith, or *is not every article of belief choked and poisoned with a sophism?*" (p. 19.) "Oh, it is agony enough to have felt or seen such things; . . . . setting the *seal of falsehood* on foreheads once open and pure and true, ... We prevaricate and evade and get out of difficulties, in a manner *worthy of those whose rule of faith is the Catholic interpretation which Tractarianism puts on the Prayer-book and Articles of our Reformed Church.*" (p. 26.)

Now these are *not*, it must be observed, *my words*. They are the expressions extorted by the upbraidings of conscience from warm adherents of the party; wrung from them by the agonized feelings that resulted from a comparison of their real principles with their professions, their secret views and practices with their public avowals. And there can hardly, I think, be more genuine and striking evidence as to the true character of Tractarianism than is afforded by this spontaneous outburst of feeling respecting it from one of its disciples.*

* I am quite aware that an endeavour has been made to raise a *tu quoque* argument against the Evangelical party on this ground, on account of their denial of the doctrine of Baptismal Regeneration, which their opponents hold that the Prayer Book teaches; and that this argument has also been urged against them in other quarters. The only reply which it seems to me at all necessary *now* to make to such accusations, and a very sufficient reply to all the lucubrations of newspaper editors, and writers in reviews, the dogmatism of Romanizers, the anti-church prejudices of dissenters, and the ignorance of historical theology (to which the question belongs) in some members of our Church, lay and clerical, is to point such cavillers first to the known views of the compilers of our Formularies, and more especially to the Judgment pronounced, after a long, careful, and elaborate investigation of the matter, by some of the ablest legal minds in the kingdom,—known to have been previously somewhat inclined in the opposite direction,—in the case of Gorham *v.* the Bishop of Exeter; followed up, it may be added, by the frank and public admission of one who was an earnest adviser of the movement on the part of the Bishop, that the course of the discussion had produced in him the conviction that the doctrine of Baptismal Regeneration, for which he had been contending, was not that of the Church of England.

After an elaborate settlement of the question of this kind, to see second or third-rate writers or speakers laying down the law on the subject, and uttering denunciations against those who do not view the matter in the light in which it appears to them, is only calculated to raise a smile. In such a case it is a work of supererogation to re-argue the matter. It is enough to ask such parties one question,—Are you better able to pass a judgment on this matter than those who, after a long and elaborate investigation of it, delivered the above-mentioned Judgment? And I may add, that this seems to me a sufficient reply to all the pulpit denunciations and newspaper articles which appeared not long since upon the subject, and which, being as utterly powerless to shake that Judgment as the spray of the ocean to move the rocks, it would have been a waste of time to notice.

In connection with this point, I may add a remark on the recent boast of Dr. Pusey, echoed by others of his party, that those who "disbelieve in baptismal regeneration, or in their orders, have for some time been steadily

For my own part, I am satisfied to let the party be judged by the principles which they themselves have openly avowed. And all I say to the public is, Observe that their teaching is founded upon the doctrine of "*economy*," that speaks the truth EXCEPT when the interests of supposed orthodoxy require the contrary. They can belong, therefore, outwardly to a Protestant Church, while in heart they are Romanists; proclaim their *ex animo* consent to Protestant Formularies, and explain them as meaning Romish doctrines; and by means of their subscription to those Formularies, use the revenues and privileges of a Protestant Church for the purpose of effecting its overthrow, and bringing about its re-incorporation into the Church which those Formularies proclaim to be apostate and corrupt. It is for the public to judge whether this form of Christianity, which we may, without giving reasonable cause of offence, denominate the "economical" form, commends itself to their approval, and whether they are willing to allow its supporters to work out the ends they have proposed to themselves.

I do not for a moment deny their zeal or piety or reli-

---

diminishing." (Letter to the "Literary Churchman.") The bolder spirits of his party, indeed, are assuring the public that Evangelicalism is comparatively dead, almost a thing of the past. Nothing is more easy than to make such assertions, and of course the doctrine of "economy" allows them to be made *ad libitum;* and Dr. Pusey and his party have from the first largely availed themselves of the privilege. I will venture, however, to remind Dr. Pusey of a fact which he may have forgotten, and which I will avail myself of this opportunity of leaving on record. After the delivery of the *Gorham Judgment*, the Tractarian Journals, burning with indignation, represented the clergy as with very few exceptions resenting and reprobating the Judgment with a feeling of warm disapprobation. Under the circumstances of that period, it seemed worth while to shew the public how far this statement was correct, and accordingly a Declaration was issued testifying "thankfulness for the Judgment" as "a wise and just Sentence, in accordance with the principles of the Church of England," and this Declaration, although only *partially* distributed among the clergy, was signed by more than *three thousand two hundred and sixty* of them, including seven Deans, thirteen Archdeacons, and more than twenty Canons. A Declaration of an opposite kind, *sent to every name on the Clergy List, and to a large number of the laity,* received only, I was informed, about seventeen hundred signatures, including both clergy and laity, and was *very prudently* never suffered to appear before the public; and for a time the Thrasonic boasts of the party were hushed. But it seems that the weapon is too valuable to be permanently disused, and everything is allowable that tends to advance "Catholic" doctrines, and promote the interests of "Mother Church."

giousness, *according to their form of Christianity:* but I do deny, that their form is *Christ's form of Christianity,* the Christianity of the New Testament, either in its *moral* or its *dogmatic* aspect. I agree with a remark I recollect meeting with somewhere, (though I cannot at this moment recall the exact place, and therefore attach no authority to the reference,) made by a Roman Catholic prelate at the time of the Reformation, on first perusing the New Testament, *to this effect,*—If this is Christ's religion, ours is not so. The "sacramental system," as held by the Church of Rome and the Romanizing party in our Church, to say nothing of the dogmas of saint-worship, prayer for the dead, and other similar corruptions of the faith that generally in time grow out of it, is as alien to the Christian faith, as taught by Christ and His Apostles in the New Testament, as the precept of "speaking falsely" for the sake of promoting the interests of Christ's Church is opposed to the purity of its morality. But I repeat, that I agree in all the encomiums passed in certain quarters, which I need not name, upon the earnestness of their religiousness, provided that they be understood to apply to *their form of Christianity.* But I must at the same time add,— God forbid that their form of Christianity, either as respects its morals or its dogmas, should be that adopted by the people of this country. And in so speaking I am using language far less strong than that which is applied to portions of that system by the Articles and Homilies of our Church; whose declarations all the clergy of our Church, *its Bishops especially,* are bound to uphold.

The comparative impunity with which the Tractarian party have been allowed to introduce their doctrines and practices into our Church, has, as might have been expected, produced a state of things which seriously threatens the peace of the country. The attempts to explain away our Formularies, to secretly encourage Romish views and practices, to stealthily introduce Popish fittings into our churches, and stigmatize the doctrines restored to the Church by the Reformation as "*extreme views,*" have been succeeded by open abuse of those Formularies and of those who give them the meaning they (as it is *admitted*) were intended to bear, and a bold adoption of Romish rites and practices and services that have changed the appearance of many of our Protestant churches so that they are scarcely distinguishable from those of Rome.* Finding that the reins of Church government were, as it were, flung over their necks, they have adopted their own will as their law; and by the flimsy device of a pretended obedience to imaginary supreme laws of the "Catholic Church," have set at defiance those of their own Church, which their own vows and promises bound them to observe.

To judge of their regard for the Prayer-book, especially the Communion Service, (which indeed was long ago said by one of the party to be "a judgment on the Church,"†) we need not go further than the Essays of the Rev. S. Baring-Gould and the Rev. Orby Shipley, in the volume entitled "The Church and the World," recently published under the editorship of the latter. It is painful to have to add, that this volume was presented publicly in Convocation by the Bishop of Oxford to the Archbishop of Canterbury, with, to say the least, no words of disapprobation of its contents.

The language, indeed, which has been used by some of the Tractarian party with respect to parts of the Prayer-book, strongly reminds one of the direction given to the Romish

---

* This is broadly avowed. Thus writes the Rev. E. L. Blenkinsopp, in "The Church and the World":—"Anglicans are reproached by Protestants with their resemblance to Romans: they say a stranger entering into a church where Ritual is carefully attended to, might easily mistake it for a Roman service. OF COURSE HE MIGHT; *the whole purpose of the great revival has been to eliminate the dreary Protestantism of the Hanoverian period, and restore the glory of Catholic worship. Our churches are restored after the mediæval pattern, and our Ritual must accord with the Catholic standard.* . . . Ritual, like painting and architecture, is only the visible expression of Divine truth. Without dogma, without *on esoteric meaning*, Ritual is an illusion and a delusion: a lay figure without life or spirit, a *vox et præterea nihil.* The experience of the last century shows, that it is impossible to preserve the Catholic faith excepting by Catholic Ritual; the experience of the present century equally makes manifest the fact, that the revival of the Catholic faith must be accompanied by the revival of Catholic Ritual; and still more, *that the surest way to teach the Catholic faith is by Catholic Ritual.*" (2nd ed. pp. 212, 213).

† Froude's Remains. See also Newman's Letter to Fausset, 2nd ed. pp. 46, 47; and Mr. Keble's Preface to Hooker, p. lxii.

emissaries in the beginning of Queen Elizabeth's reign, that if the offer to confirm the Liturgy, "*with some things altered therein,*" and with the acknowledgment that it was used under the Pope's authority, was not accepted, then they were "to asperse the Liturgy of England by all ways and conspiracies imaginable."*

As a specimen of the language now used respecting the Thirty-nine Articles, I content myself with the following extract from a recent number of the *Christian Remembrancer:*—

"When it is considered that the Articles were drawn up at a time when *theology had reached nearly its lowest level* in the Church of England, and were remodelled after the accession of Elizabeth, when the tone of religious belief was *still lower*, one is really tempted to ask with wonder, How is it that men have placed such implicit belief in them? And no other answer can be given than that they have been neglected and ignored. Of course there has been a large party who swear by them, *and the existence of whose form of belief in the Church of England is guaranteed by their being retained;* but it is impossible to deny, that they contain statements or implications that are *verbally false,* and others that are *very difficult to reconcile with truth.* In the times that are coming over the Church of England, the question will arise, What service have the Articles of the Church of England ever done? and of what use are they at the present day? The latter question must be answered very fully and satisfactorily, if the answer is to be any make-weight against the condemnation of them virtually pronounced by the *Eirenicon* [*i. e.* of Dr. Pusey]. . . . . We venture to go a step beyond any suggestion contained in this volume, and boldly proclaim our own opinion, that before union with Rome can be effected, the Thirty-nine Articles must be *wholly withdrawn.* They *are virtually withdrawn* at the present moment."†

These are the words of one of the leading organs of the

---
* See p. 11 above.
† Review of Dr. Pusey's Eirenicon, in the Christian Remembrancer for Jan. 1866, p. 188.

Tractarian party; and they are but a specimen of their present tone.

Such are the allies which the Church of Rome now possesses in our own Church. For more than thirty years they have been allowed, almost without let or hindrance from the Authorities of our Church, (for *mere words* of rebuke and remonstrance are valueless when it is known that they will under no circumstances be followed by *acts*,) to indoctrinate the public mind with their views, to train up a set of "priests" openly claiming all the sacerdotal powers assumed by the Romish priesthood, and so steeped in that system of morals which from the first has characterized Tractarianism that they can sign their *ex animo* consent to Protestant Formularies, drawn up, as is admitted, for the maintenance and defence of Protestant doctrine, in order to get a *locus standi* in a Protestant Church, with the intention of teaching the opposite doctrine, and on the first opportunity abolishing those Formularies and transforming the Church into which they have thus stolen from a Protestant to a Popish Church.

The mask under cover of which Tractarianism commenced its labours has now been torn from it. It was, I admit, but a transparent mask, a flimsy veil, to those who knew anything of the real principles of Popery. But it accomplished its end—the deception of the multitude, until it could boast a party that made it safe to act with less disguise. And now it stands forth as Rome's staunch ally. It may for the present be shy in its advances, and pretend to haggle about the *conditions* of reconciliation; but no one except a willing dupe can be deceived by this.

We have been lately warned against a "*self-satisfied* Calvinism," and asked to admire the piety and zeal of those who are thus promoting the cause of Popery among us. But I think there are some, who are not Calvinists, who will hold, that such men as Archbishops Whitgift and Usher, and Bishops Hall, Davenant, and Morton, are not much inferior to the examples to which we are here pointed; and who will at least think it unfortunate, that one who is contented thus to rebuke the views and spirit of such theologians, should select for his special reproof their supposed spirit of *self-satisfaction*.

I commend to the consideration of the author of this warning the admonition once addressed by one whom I am sure he will consider entitled to his respect, Dr. Phillpotts, now Bishop of Exeter, to a celebrated statesman who had spoken slightingly of " Calvinists" :—

" To the peculiar tenets of that denomination of Christians, to which you appear to allude, I am very far from subscribing; but thus much I will say, that *no man, who knows what they really are, will ever treat them with contempt.* You, Sir, do not appear to have yet risen above THE VULGAREST PREJUDICES on this subject; else *you would have known, that opinions which have commended themselves to the full and firm conviction of* SOME OF THE ABLEST AS WELL AS HOLIEST MEN WHO HAVE EVER ADORNED OUR CHURCH, *are not to be thus blown down by 'the whiff and wind' of the smartest piece of rhetoric ever discharged in your honourable House."*

The term, however, as used in the quarter to which I have referred, is simply a term of reproach taken up as a controversial weapon against those of a different school of theology, as the name *Puritan* was applied in former times; for it is a complete misnomer in the case of many of those against whom it is directed.

There is, I fear, an erroneous notion entertained in some quarters respecting this movement in our Church, which the evidence given above will I trust suffice to remove. It is imagined that it has arisen from a mere accidental and temporary outburst of Romish proclivities on the part of certain zealous members of our Church, of a peculiar idiosyncrasy, which may have its day and then subside. There cannot be a greater fallacy. It is a revival of a movement, the fruit of Romish intrigue, which is only part of a conspiracy against our Church as the chief bulwark of the Reformation,

* Dr. Phillpotts's Letter to the Right Hon. G. Canning. Lond. 1825; pp. 106, 107.

having its root and centre of operations at Rome, and its ramifications, consisting of agencies of various kinds and descriptions, pervading the land—a conspiracy that has been in existence almost from the Reformation to the present day, varying in activity and strength according as the circumstances of the times favoured or not its development. The view taken of it by those who look at it merely as an individual and local effort, apart from the great movement of which it forms but a branch, must necessarily be of the most superficial and inadequate kind.

The dangers of the present times are greatly increased by their being so much overlooked; and any attempt to make the public conscious of them is resented by many as a false alarm. For what above all things is desired by the Tractarian party is, to be allowed quietly to leaven the Church with their views, as teachers of the genuine doctrine of the Church of England, "the principles of the Church."* And therefore, though they boast of the "mighty movement"† they have originated, the "struggle"‡ in which they are engaged, they complain of being dealt with as agitators, and plaintively exclaim, "What we long for ..... is at the least peace."§

It now remains to be seen how far the country is prepared to allow the efforts of Rome, and her allies in the Church of England, to bring our Church and nation once more under subjection to the Pope, to be crowned with success.

Let it not be supposed, that Rome will ever be satisfied with anything less than what she has all along been contending for; *supreme dominion* over the faith of the country. And how that dominion would be used, we have been lately told by the Pope himself. It must never be forgotten by those who would not shut their eyes to the real principles and objects of the Church of Rome, maintained at the present day equally as at any former period, that the Pope

---

* Pusey's Letter to Abp. of Cant., p. 29.   ‡ Ib. p. 84.
† Ib. p. 136.   § Ib. p. 136.

himself, in his Encyclical Letter of Dec. 8, 1864, has formally condemned, as one of the "principal *errors* of our time," the proposition that "in the present day it is no longer expedient that the [Roman] Catholic religion should be considered as the only religion of the State, *to the exclusion of all other forms of worship.*"* And for a fuller explanation of his meaning on this point, he referred to an "Allocution" he had delivered July 26, 1855, in which, speaking of Spain, he had said,—"You know that in the year 1851 we concluded a convention with our dear daughter in Jesus Christ, the Queen of Spain, and that among its various provisions which affected the Catholic religion we especially stipulated, that this holy religion should continue to be the only religion of the Spanish nation, *to the exclusion of all other worship, and that in all schools, whether public or private, the instruction should be entirely conformed to Catholic doctrine.*"

The advance of Popery, therefore, among us is a matter which seriously affects the interests of others besides members of the Church of England. The absorption of the National Church into the vortex of the corrupt Church of Rome could not fail to have a vast influence upon the state of the Dissenting Communions in this country. The Nonconformists may flatter themselves that they are too numerous and powerful to be injured by the re-establishment of Popery as the National Church. But it would be well for them to recollect, that in such an Establishment they would have a very different sort of rival to deal with than what they now have; and that the active agency of Rome, enjoying the advantages of such a position, would subject them to dangers and difficulties of which they have now no experience. To say nothing of the treatment that would be accorded to them, the moment that the Romish party felt itself strong enough to carry out its principles and accomplish its designs, the very presence, side by side with them, of a National Church presenting to their members every attraction by which the

---

* Ætate hac nostra non amplius expedit, religionem catholicam haberi tamquam unicam Status religionem, ceteris quibuscumque cultibus exclusis. Alloc. *Nemo vestrum.* 26 Julii, 1855.

senses of mankind can be allured, utterly unscrupulous in its mode of gaining proselytes, and bent upon bringing the whole nation under its sway, would be an ever-present danger constantly imperilling their very existence. Certain it is, that Rome has always believed, that if the National Church again became hers, she could make comparatively short work with the sects. I am not so sure of this, because I believe she would reap the fruits of her own wickedness in scattering discord and false doctrine over the land, and find that it is easier to produce strife and variance, than force upon mankind a constrained concord. But this much at least is clear, that the restored ascendancy of Popery in this country would bring manifold dangers upon every Protestant Communion existing within it.

There is much in Popery, especially as presented to the view of a Protestant nation whom it desires to conciliate, that is attractive to the minds of the generality:—the splendour and beauty of its ceremonial, the power it claims to decide all controversies, and thus deliver the Church from all the strifes and divisions by which its peace is disturbed, the right it assumes to itself as a Divine gift to restore peace to the troubled conscience of the penitent, on the confession of his sin, by an authoritative absolution, and open the gate of heaven to the dying—all these are recommendations for its acceptance which, when brought home to the very doors of families, many of whose members are necessarily but imperfectly grounded in the faith, can hardly fail to influence many minds.

It comes moreover to many in this land at the present day with all the charms of novelty. The form which it assumes in a Protestant country so conceals many of its worst features, that the minds of the great mass of the community, especially of the young and inexperienced, hardly recognize in it what they had expected. The lessons of history, if known, (and few comparatively *do* know them,) are forgotten or ignored. And it is hastily concluded, that Popery has either been very much misrepresented, or is very much changed.

All the various Protestant Communions, therefore, have a common interest in preventing Rome's designs being crowned with success.

It may be expected, that, before I conclude, I should make a few remarks on the way in which the dangers with which we are threatened should be met. But my object in these pages is rather to call attention to the light which our past history affords as to the nature of those dangers, and the aid it gives us to read the signs of the present times. The question as to the best mode of meeting those dangers, is one the *public discussion* of which is not likely to be of much service. And past experience makes it but a melancholy task to repeat the oft-urged warning as to the peril in which our Church is placed by the wiles of Rome and her allies among ourselves.

Let us look at what has been taking place in our own Church.

It is now more than a quarter of a century since the leaders of the Romanizing movement in the English Church warned the nation of the object they had in view. Mr. Newman, in Tract XC., lately republished with high commendations by Dr. Pusey, while affirming that the Thirty-nine Articles were "the offspring of an *un-Catholic* age," and admitting that they were "drawn up by Protestants, and intended for the establishment of Protestantism," at the same time urged their not being interpreted according to "the known opinions of their framers," but in a "*Catholic*" sense. Dr. Pusey, in his Letter to the Archbishop of Canterbury, intimated, that our Church had been possessed of an evil spirit ever since the Reformation, which it would be their endeavour to cast out; that what, in imitation of the unscrupulous policy of Rome, he designated as the "*Genevan* scheme of doctrine," introduced into our Church by our Reformers, was to be rooted out to make way for the "*Catholic* scheme of doctrine;" and that the "struggle" for effecting these objects would be continued by them until it had a decisive issue; and he likened it to the struggle which takes place in a *demoniac*, when the *evil spirit* is cast out of "*the body it has possessed.*"

What has been *done* to vindicate the principles of the Reformation, and rescue our Church from the dangers with which it has thus been threatened? Nothing! Words of admonition, indeed, have not been wanting. Eli's warning to his sons may have been administered by many, and is still heard in some quarters, mixed with the language of sympathy and praise. But what is *most wanted*, and what alone can be *effectual*,—the legal prevention of the inculcation of such doctrine by Ministers of our Church—has not only not been attempted, but, when attempted by others, has been resisted. The simple reply to those who fear to bring the matter before our tribunals is, If the Formularies of our Church are not distinct enough to condemn the doctrines of the Tractarian party, we have no right to find fault with them for teaching those doctrines. But I know by experience that what above all things that party deprecate is, to have their doctrine brought to the test of judicial investigation.* They know well that the mode of explaining away the Articles taught by Tract XC., and by which alone they are enabled to retain their position in the Church of England, would not be listened to in a court of law. The case of Archdeacon Denison gave full proof of this. Every possible effort was made to prevent that case coming before a court of law. Influences of all kinds, high in Church and State, were put in motion by leaders of the party, to stop its progress. The Bishop of the Diocese, refusing to act

---

* No such feeling has existed on the other side. On the contrary, such a test of the consistency of the doctrines of what is called "the Evangelical party" with the Formularies of the Church of England has been courted. So far from there being any desire to shrink from submitting their doctrine on the effects of Baptism (their opponents' chief charge against them) to judicial investigation, the opportunity of doing so was gladly embraced; and an overture of better preferment made for the purpose of stopping the legal appeal declined, from the resolution to have the question legally settled.

on the advice of his Ecclesiastical Superior, and send the case to the Court of Arches, illegally constituted himself the Judge, and with a mockery of justice pretended to pass sentence on it himself. His successor repeated the refusal to let the case be fairly tried.* The Archdeacon himself, when obliged to appear before a Commission, refused to acknowledge himself to be the author of sermons which he had preached in the cathedral, and which had been published and circulated by himself. And through the delay thus caused, chiefly by the refusal of the Bishops even to let the case be *tried*, though at the expense of other parties, when the condemnatory sentence of the Lower Court came up to the Judicial Committee of the Privy Council for confirmation, it was found that the case had been delayed beyond the time prescribed by the Act.

The reason for this shrinking from a Judicial Sentence is obvious. A legal Judgment delivered by those accustomed to weigh evidence and give sentence accordingly, grounded upon the Formularies of our Church drawn up by the divines of the Reformation, must, as they well know, go against them. And therefore they wish to keep all such matters in the hands of *clerical partisans*, who, instead of acting with judicial impartiality upon the documents that ought to be their supreme and sole guide, attempt to force upon Reformation Formularies a doctrine which they profess to derive from what *they call* " Catholic consent" and the tradition of the early Church, but which is, in fact, a Romish corruption of Apostolic doctrine, and which they at times admit that those Formularies were not intended to teach.

A secret guiding principle of the movement for many years has been to prevent legal decisions upon its doctrines, until, by

---

* It is a remarkable fact, that at the time when the new school of doctrine was rising in our Church, the Bishops got an Act passed, called the Church Discipline Act, by which a power was placed in their hands that had never before been given to them, and which I believe the laity under present circumstances would not have granted to them, namely, that no proceedings can be taken against any clergyman but through them and with their sanction. And *the power was immediately abused*, as stated above.

the aid of earnest adherents and noisy agitators acting through the various channels of the Press, well-organized Societies, and such like instruments, a step in advance can be gained, either by getting the XXXIX. Articles altered, or by subscription to them being relaxed in such a way that the Ecclesiastical Courts will be powerless for maintaining Protestant doctrine in our Church. *It is of essential importance to the success of any efforts to counteract the movement, to keep this in view.*

The subtle influences that are at work in our Church in all directions to effect a change in its doctrine and worship, are more dangerous enemies to its welfare than even the operations, open or secret, of the Papists. And the public little know, how wily and indefatigable are the efforts of many influential parties in high position, apparently keeping themselves aloof from the Tractarian movement, and even administering occasionally to its partisans certain prudent and harmless reproofs, to undo the work of the Reformation and re-found our Church on what Dr. Pusey would call the " Catholic Scheme of doctrine."

Among the suggestions that have lately been made for meeting the difficulties of the present crisis, one is, that application should be made for a Royal Commission to give advice on the subject. I confess that, to say nothing of the delay thus caused, my hopes of a satisfactory result from the deliberations of such a body would be *very small*.

So far, indeed, as concerns a Royal Commission for the purpose for which some have recently desired it, namely, *the revision of the Prayer Book in some of its Services*, I can imagine nothing more undesirable, except perhaps *the request for it*.

Anything more suicidal, under the circumstances in which our Church has been placed for the last thirty years, than to be putting a Romish interpretation upon passages in the Prayer Book, which we know was never meant by our Reformers who compiled it, and agitating for their revision, can hardly be conceived. I know nothing, indeed, that has done more damage to the cause of Protestantism in our Church than this unwise movement. It was, in fact, a favourite weapon with the disguised agents of Rome. One of the chief topics in the discourses of the concealed Jesuits in the beginning of Queen Elizabeth's reign, referred to above,* for the purpose of producing disaffection to the Church, and consequent division and strife among the people, was, that the Prayer Book was *not sufficiently reformed.*

Whether some phrases in the Prayer Book best express *in the present day* what our Reformers intended to be understood by them, is an abstract question which men may hold their own opinion about; but to damage the peace and welfare of the whole Church for the sake of carrying out a private opinion on this subject, is to sacrifice the interests of thousands for the satisfaction of individual feelings and scruples. It is hardly fair, indeed, for a small subdivision of a large body to attempt to subject the interests of that body to an influence which it would deprecate and by which it might be seriously damaged.

The wisdom of an application to Parliament depends altogether upon considerations and circumstances which it would be undesirable to discuss in these pages. Would that we had there the Protestant feeling which, as we see from the foregoing pages, was, under God, the means of saving this country in former times from the curse of Popery. I would fain hope, however, that there is enough of the feeling left in that body to make it unwilling to see the National Church again overspread with the corrupt doctrines and practices from which the Reformation delivered us.

As concerns the efforts of individuals, much no doubt may be done through the pulpit, the press, and the platform. But if any effectual opposition is contemplated to the advances of Popery, it must be by united, steady, persevering, general, and well-organized efforts, very different from the timid, desultory, spasmodic, individual movements

---

* See pp. 13—15 above.

within which our Protestantism has as yet confined itself. We may take a hint on this point from our opponents' policy, while we repudiate its concomitants. Their rule is, Little talk and much action; little noise and commotion, much quiet organization, arrangement, and influence; unity in the source of action, sacrifice of individual feelings, co-operation with one object in view, and a host of different and widely-scattered agencies simultaneously at work to accomplish it. Such a movement, originating in a centre of action and counsel, possessing judgment and experience, working by affiliated agencies pervading the country, and co-operating to a common end through mutual consultation and correspondence, can do more than all the efforts of isolated individuals, or of bodies guided by the discordant counsels of members of different views and feelings, can ever effect.

But it can no longer be doubted, that if a vigorous national effort is not at once made to arrest the course of the movement which Rome and her allies among ourselves have raised in this country, the aspect of our Church will be altogether changed, and its Protestantism be a thing of the past.

Are we willing quietly to permit this result to be achieved? Are we ready to drop the Protestant banner, and calmly allow *Ichabod* to be inscribed on our Reformed Church? Surely not. The inheritance of a pure form of faith and worship, obtained for us, through God's mercy, by the blood of our martyred forefathers, is a trust committed to our keeping by One who will hold us responsible for casting it away from us.

They were not, let us hope, vain, but *prophetic,* words that flowed from the lips of our noble Latimer, as he stood at the stake,—" Be of good comfort, Master Ridley, and play the man; we shall this day light such a candle by God's grace in England, as, I trust,

SHALL NEVER BE PUT OUT."